How to Use This Book

Look for these special features in this book:

SIDEBARS, **CHARTS**, **GRAPHS**, and original **MAPS** expand your understanding of what's being discussed—and also make useful sources for classroom reports.

FAQs answer common **F**requently **A**sked **Q**uestions about people, places, and things.

WOW FACTORS offer "Who knew?" facts to keep you thinking.

TRAVEL GUIDE gives you tips on exploring the state—either in person or right from your chair!

PROJECT ROOM provides fun ideas for school assignments and incredible research projects. Plus, there's a guide to primary sources—what they are and how to cite them.

Please note: All statistics are as up-to-date as possible at the time of publication. Population data is taken from the 2010 census.

Consultants: William Loren Katz; Gary Kremer, Executive Director, The State Historical Society of Missouri; Cheryl Seeger, Missouri State Geologist; Lisa Gilbert, M.A.

Book production by The Design Lab

Library of Congress Cataloging-in-Publication Data
Blashfield, Jean F.
 Missouri / by Jean F. Blashfield. — Revised edition.
 pages cm. — (America the beautiful, third series)
 Includes bibliographical references and index.
 Audience: Ages 9–12.
 ISBN 978-0-531-28282-3 (lib. bdg. : alk. paper)
 1. Missouri—Juvenile literature. I. Title.
 F466.3.B58 2014
 977.8—dc23   2013044325

1 2 3 4 5 6 7 8 9 10 R 24 23 22 21 20 19 18 17 16 15

Revised Edition

AMERICA ★ THE ★ BEAUTIFUL

Missouri

BY JEAN F. BLASHFIELD

Third Series, Revised Edition

Children's Press®
An Imprint of Scholastic Inc.
New York ★ Toronto ★ London ★ Auckland ★ Sydney
Mexico City ★ New Delhi ★ Hong Kong
Danbury, Connecticut

CONTENTS

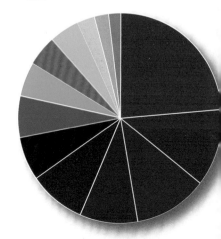

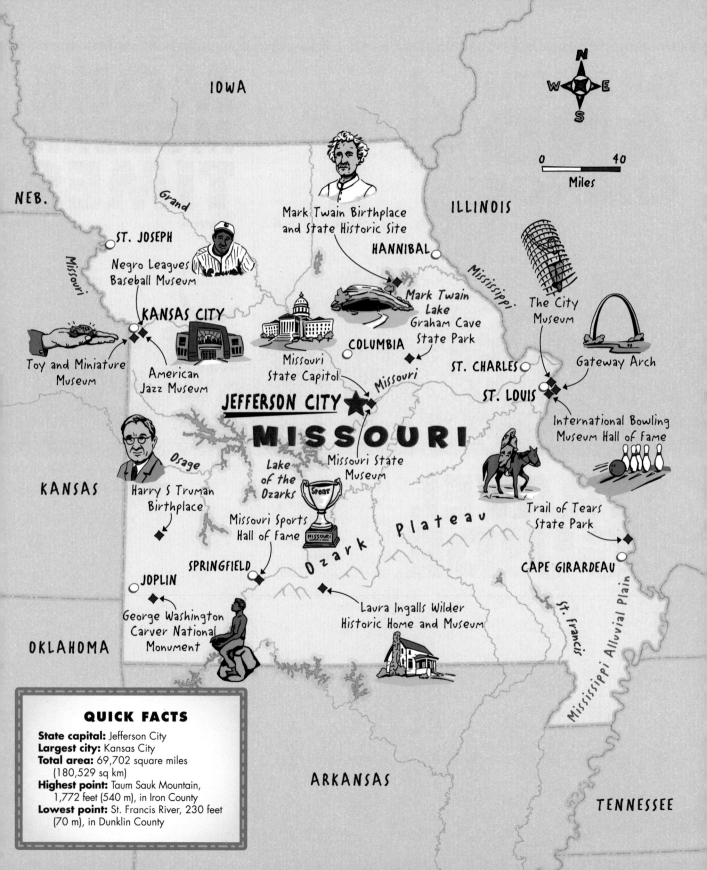

IOWA

NEB.

ILLINOIS

Mark Twain Birthplace
and State Historic Site

HANNIBAL

N
W E
S

0   40
Miles

ST. JOSEPH

Negro Leagues
Baseball Museum

Grand

Missouri

KANSAS CITY

Mark Twain
Lake
Graham Cave
State Park

COLUMBIA

The City
Museum

Mississippi

Toy and Miniature
Museum

American
Jazz Museum

Missouri
State Capitol

ST. CHARLES

Missouri

ST. LOUIS

Gateway Arch

JEFFERSON CITY ★

MISSOURI

Missouri State
Museum

International Bowling
Museum Hall of Fame

KANSAS

Harry S Truman
Birthplace

Osage

Lake
of the
Ozarks

Sport

Missouri Sports
Hall of Fame

MISSOURI

Ozark   Plateau

Trail of Tears
State Park

CAPE GIRARDEAU

SPRINGFIELD

St. Francis

JOPLIN

George Washington
Carver National
Monument

Laura Ingalls Wilder
Historic Home and Museum

Mississippi Alluvial Plain

OKLAHOMA

ARKANSAS

TENNESSEE

QUICK FACTS

State capital: Jefferson City
Largest city: Kansas City
Total area: 69,702 square miles
(180,529 sq km)
Highest point: Taum Sauk Mountain,
1,772 feet (540 m), in Iron County
Lowest point: St. Francis River, 230 feet
(70 m), in Dunklin County

Welcome to Missouri!

HOW DID MISSOURI GET ITS NAME?

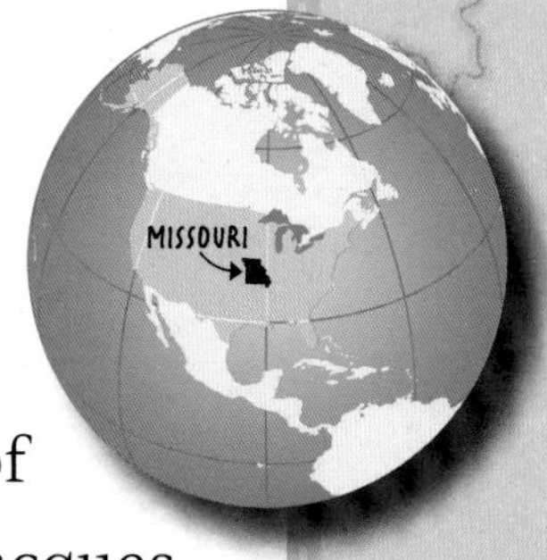

The Mesquakie (also called Fox) people, who lived along the Mississippi River, had neighbors who rowed large canoes. They called them *Oumessourit*, which means "people of the big canoes." The early French explorers Jacques Marquette and Louis Jolliet tried to spell out the name they heard. Over the centuries, the European pronunciation and spelling of the Indian word changed as different explorers and settlers came into the region. The spelling became "Missouri," but even today people disagree about the pronunciation. Some Missourians say "miz-UHR-uh," while others say "miz-UHR-ee."

MISSOURI

WEST VIRGINIA

VIRGINIA

ILLINOIS

KENTUCKY

NORTH CAROLINA

TENNESSEE

SOUTH CAROLINA

8

READ ABOUT

Kayakers paddle
on the Lake of
the Ozarks.

CHAPTER ONE

LAND

★

MISSOURI IS LOCATED NEAR THE MIDDLE OF THE UNITED STATES. So is it a western state or an eastern one? Is it northern or southern? Missouri serves as a crossroads and a borderland, connecting all of those regions. Missouri spreads across 69,702 square miles (180,529 square kilometers). Taum Sauk Mountain rises to 1,772 feet (540 meters) above sea level in the southeastern part of the state. It is Missouri's highest peak. The state's lowest point, 230 feet (70 m) along the St. Francis River, is also in the southeast.

Fishers enjoy the sunset along the Missouri River.

Eight states border Missouri, which ties with Tennessee for having the most neighboring states.

LOCATING MISSOURI

Missouri has an unusual shape, because some of its borders follow natural features. To the east, the Mississippi River defines its border with Illinois, Kentucky, and Tennessee. The southern border is with Arkansas. Most of this border is a straight line, but an area that looks like the heel of a boot, known as the Bootheel region, juts farther south. To the west are Nebraska, Kansas, and Oklahoma. The Missouri River forms the jagged northern part of this border. The northern border with Iowa is mostly another straight line.

LAND REGIONS

Missouri can be divided into four land regions. The regions' names tell you what kind of landscape to expect.

Dissected Till Plains

Great sheets of ice called **glaciers** covered the Dissected **Till** Plains at least five different times, most recently about 11,500 years ago. Thus this region, now northern Missouri, is also known as the Glacial Plains. The glaciers flattened the land, producing plains. When the last ice sheet retreated, it left gravel and soil, called till, in its wake. In Missouri, the till is about 25 to 100 feet (7.6 to 30 m) thick. The rivers and streams formed by water that melted off the glaciers carved up, or dissected, the plains.

WORDS TO KNOW

glaciers *slow-moving masses of ice*

till *the gravel and soil left behind after a glacier retreats*

Missouri Geo-Facts

Along with the state's geographical highlights, this chart ranks Missouri's land, water, and total area compared to all other states.

Total area; rank . . . . . 69,702 square miles (180,529 sq km); 21st
Land; rank . . . . .68,716 square miles (177,974 sq km); 18th
Water; rank . . . . .987 square miles (2,556 sq km); 32nd
Inland water; rank . . . . 987 square miles (2,556 sq km); 24th
Geographic center . . . . Miller County, 20 miles (32 km) southwest of Jefferson City
Latitude . . . . .36° N to 40°35′ N
Longitude . . . . 89°6′ W to 95°42′ W
Highest point . . . . Taum Sauk Mountain, 1,772 feet (540 m), in Iron County
Lowest point . . . . .St. Francis River, 230 feet (70 m), in Dunklin County
Largest city . . . . Kansas City
Longest river . . . . . . .Missouri River, 175 miles (282 km) in Missouri

Source: U.S. Census Bureau, 2010 census

Rhode Island, the nation's smallest state, would fit inside Missouri 45 times.

Onondaga Cave formations in the Ozarks

WORD TO KNOW

plateau *an elevated part of the earth with steep slopes*

The Ozark National Scenic Riverways was the first national park area created to protect a wild river system. It protects both the Current and Jacks Fork rivers, along with many caves and springs.

The Ozark Plateau

About 250 million years ago, pressure below the earth's crust thrust up the Ozark **Plateau**, an area that now lies south of the Missouri River. The Ozark Plateau was once under an ocean. For many millions of years, seashells sank to the ocean floor. They were eventually compressed into layers of limestone hundreds of feet thick. After the ocean disappeared, the limestone was on the surface. Because limestone is a soft rock, rainwater and underground springs carved many caves in it.

Parts of the Ozark Plateau are called Cave Country. Waterfalls flow among the formations in Crystal Cave near Springfield. Its walls sparkle with crystals. Marble Cave is near the Arkansas border. It includes one room in which sound carries perfectly, just as it does in the world's greatest concert halls.

As the plateau's soft rock eroded, or wore away, areas of hard rock were left behind. These raised areas that didn't erode are now the Ozark Mountains. They are among the oldest mountains in North America. Among the peaks and valleys of the Ozarks meanders the shallow Gasconade River. It is the longest (and probably most twisty) river lying completely in Missouri. It flows 265 miles (426 km) from its source in the southwest near Hartville to where it empties into the Missouri River.

The rugged St. Francois Mountains are also in the Ozark Upland. These mountains were once large volcanic craters. The volcanoes died out about 1.2 billion years ago. The craters slowly eroded into mountains and were covered by **sedimentary** rock. When the Ozark Plateau was uplifted, the St. Francois Mountains were also uplifted and uncovered.

The highest point in the state is Taum Sauk Mountain in the St. Francois range. Near it are the oddly named Johnson's Shut-Ins. *Shut-in* is an Ozark term for a tight gorge in a stream. The gorge forms because the bed of the stream changes from softer, more easily eroded rocks to harder rocks. The stream valley is generally wider where the soft rocks make up the streambed and becomes very narrow, or shut-in, when it passes over the hard rocks. Shut-ins have lots of sculpted rock and small waterfalls.

SEE IT HERE!

MERAMEC CAVERNS

Missouri's largest cave system is Meramec Caverns in east-central Missouri. In all, the cave system covers about 26 miles (42 km). Water moving through limestone formed the caves. Dripping water also left behind mineral deposits. Drop by drop, the minerals built up into dramatic formations. Formations that hang from cave ceilings are called stalactites. Those that rise up from the cave floor are called stalagmites. Some of the formations in Meramec Caverns look like filmy curtains. Native Americans once inhabited Meramec Caverns, as did—some say—the outlaws Frank and Jesse James.

WORD TO KNOW

sedimentary *formed from clay, sand, and gravel that settled at the bottom of a body of water*

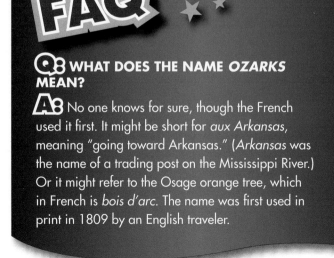

FAQ

Q8 WHAT DOES THE NAME *OZARKS* MEAN?

A8 No one knows for sure, though the French used it first. It might be short for *aux Arkansas*, meaning "going toward Arkansas." (*Arkansas* was the name of a trading post on the Mississippi River.) Or it might refer to the Osage orange tree, which in French is *bois d'arc*. The name was first used in print in 1809 by an English traveler.

Missouri Topography

Use the color-coded elevation chart to see on the map Missouri's high points (orange to yellow) and low points (green to dark green). Elevation is measured as the distance above or below sea level.

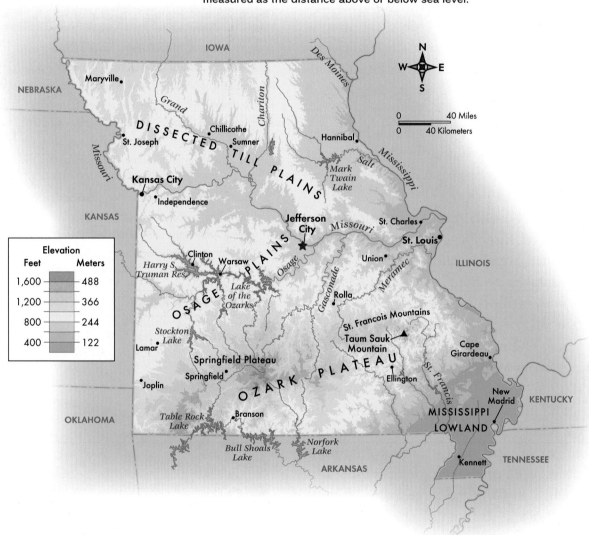

WORD TO KNOW

sediment *material eroded from rocks and deposited elsewhere by wind, water, or glaciers*

Mississippi Lowland

The Mississippi Lowland includes Missouri's Bootheel and the land just north of it. For a long time, the Mississippi River deposited **sediment** in this region when it flooded,

Sunrise over a Missouri cornfield

creating fertile farmland. Pioneers carved fields from the forests along the Mississippi and planted crops there.

The New Madrid **Fault** runs through the Bootheel. Two of the strongest earthquakes in American history occurred along this break in the earth's crust in 1811 and 1812. The quakes destroyed forests and the fields of the first white settlers in the region.

WORD TO KNOW

fault *a break in the rock deep in the earth along which earthquakes may occur*

Picture Yourself . . .

in an Earthquake

It's December 16, 1811, and you're outside cutting wood on your family's farm near the town of New Madrid. Suddenly, the earth moves under your feet. What's happening? When you see a tree start to lean toward you, you dash toward an open space. But then the earth opens up beneath you! The cabin behind you trembles and then collapses. You hear a scream and run to help your brother get out from among the fallen logs. All around you, trees are crashing to the ground, their huge roots pulled up out of the earth.

You've never heard of an earthquake, but in later years you'll learn that you experienced one of the greatest earthquakes that ever rumbled through North America. It was felt westward to the Rocky Mountains and eastward to New York and Washington, D.C. The quake even made the Mississippi River appear to flow backward for a while.

A herd of bison on a Missouri prairie

VISITING THE TALLGRASS PRAIRIE

Geographer Henry Schoolcraft, exploring Missouri's prairie in 1819, wrote: "The prairies . . . are the most extensive, rich, and beautiful of any which I have ever seen west of the Mississippi river. They are covered by a coarse wild grass, which attains so great a height that it completely hides a man on horseback in riding through it. The deer and elk abound in this quarter, and the buffalo is occasionally seen in droves upon the prairies, and in the open highland woods. Along the margin of the river, and to a width of from one to two miles each way, is found a vigorous growth of forest trees, some of which attain an almost incredible size."

Osage Plains

The Osage Plains, or Osage Prairie, is a region in south-western Missouri filled with gentle hills, rolling plains, and small forests. It is on the eastern edge of the Great Plains, a vast, generally flat area that covers the central United States. Glaciers never covered the Osage Prairie, so it does not have rich till soil like northern Missouri. Tall grasses, such as big bluestem, once grew on the Osage Prairie. Today, much of the land is used to grow corn, soy-beans, and hay, or to graze livestock.

THE BIG RIVERS

Only 818 square miles (2,119 sq km) of Missouri are water, yet the state is cradled by the largest river system in the United States, the Mississippi-Missouri system. The Mississippi River, which runs along the state's eastern border, is the nation's longest river. Its name means "great river." It begins in Minnesota and travels all the way to the Gulf of Mexico. The Missouri River (also called the Big Muddy) begins where several rivers join in Montana. By the time it crosses the middle of Missouri and joins the Mississippi at St. Louis, it is carrying enough water to double the flow of water in the great river.

Missouri National Park Areas

This map shows some of Missouri's national parks, monuments, preserves, and other areas protected by the National Park Service.

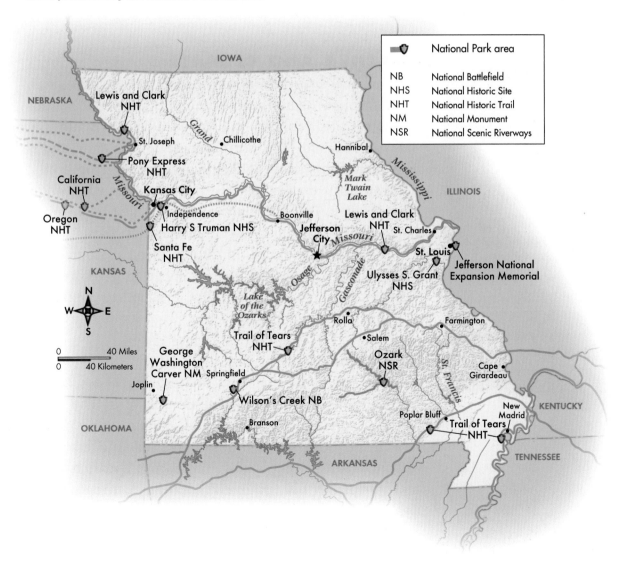

Weather Report

This chart shows record temperatures (high and low) for the state, as well as average temperatures (July and January) and average annual precipitation.

Record high temperature	118°F (48°C) at Union and Warsaw on July 14, 1954
Record low temperature	–40°F (–40°C) at Warsaw on February 13, 1905
Average July temperature, St. Louis	80°F (27°C)
Average January temperature, St. Louis	32°F (0°C)
Average yearly precipitation, St. Louis	41 inches (104 cm)

Source: National Climatic Data Center, NESDIS, NOAA, U.S. Department of Commerce

WOW

The town of Warsaw on the Lake of the Ozarks holds the records for Missouri's highest and lowest temperatures. The thermometer reached 118°F (48°C) in 1954, and dropped to –40°F (–40°C) in 1905.

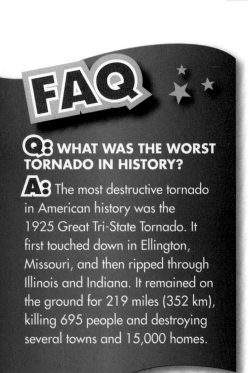

FAQ

Q8 WHAT WAS THE WORST TORNADO IN HISTORY?

A8 The most destructive tornado in American history was the 1925 Great Tri-State Tornado. It first touched down in Ellington, Missouri, and then ripped through Illinois and Indiana. It remained on the ground for 219 miles (352 km), killing 695 people and destroying several towns and 15,000 homes.

WEATHER AND CLIMATE

Missouri has hot, humid summers. Missourians often suffer through heat waves, when the temperature tops 100 degrees Fahrenheit (38 degrees Celsius). Winters in Missouri are cold. The northern part of the state sometimes gets lots of snow, while the south gets little.

Missouri is on the eastern edge of a region known as Tornado Alley. That is the area in the middle of the United States where tornadoes—some of nature's most violent storms—frequently occur. In 2011, a tornado ripped into Joplin, killing 158 people, injuring about 1,150 others, and causing $2.8 billion in damage. The tornado was the deadliest in the United States in 64 years.

PLANT LIFE

Forests cover about one-third of Missouri. These forests are mostly in the Ozarks and along rivers. The Mark Twain National Forest is scattered in nine different sections throughout 29 counties in central and southern Missouri. Settlers and lumber companies cut its original trees—primarily oak, pine, and hickory—long ago. Much of the land was replanted in seedlings during the 1930s by

A family of black bears in a Missouri forest

the Civilian Conservation Corps, a federal agency. Today, it is a diverse landscape of heavy forest and woodlands. Violets, wild roses, columbines, and goldenrods brighten the state in spring and summer.

ANIMAL LIFE

Missouri teems with all kinds of wildlife. The Ozarks are home to many kinds of creatures, including armadillos, black bears, beavers, bobcats, coyotes, opossums, otters, muskrats, deer, raccoons, skunks, squirrels, and the occasional panther.

Many kinds of birds live on the prairie, including the bobwhite quail and greater prairie chicken. Mourning doves, ruffed grouse, wild turkeys, and American wood-

ENDANGERED SPECIES

Many species in Missouri are threatened or endangered. The numbers of gray bats and Indiana bats that live in caves have dropped. The Missouri Conservation Department helps cave owners protect the bats that live within their caves.

Several endangered species make their homes in Missouri's waters. The pallid sturgeon—which is both huge, at more than 80 pounds (36 kg), and ancient (dinosaurs may have eaten it!)—swims in the Missouri and Mississippi rivers. It has been called one of the ugliest fish in North America. Not so ugly and much smaller is a tiny minnow called the Topeka shiner. It lives in prairie streams.

Indiana bats, peregrine falcons, gray wolves, and Ozark hellbenders are also endangered. The Ozark hellbender is a salamander that is found only in Missouri and Arkansas. Active at night, these amphibians may reach more than 2 feet (61 centimeters) in length!

Gray wolf

A white egret and great blue heron make a stop at the Swan Lake National Wildlife Refuge.

cocks also live in the state. Almost 50 species of ducks and geese are found in Missouri. Many more travel through the region along the Mississippi Flyway on their migrations. Swan Lake National Wildlife Refuge near Sumner is a popular stopping point for migrating waterfowl, especially snow geese.

Missouri's rivers are filled with fish such as bass, bluegill, paddlefish, and several species of whiskery catfish. The blue catfish is one of Missouri's largest fish. It can reach more than 100 pounds (45 kilograms).

PROTECTING THE ENVIRONMENT

When Europeans began to settle in the area that became Missouri, about one-third of the region was covered with prairie grasses. Today, less than 1 percent of Missouri is still prairie. As the prairies disappeared, many plants and animals that once lived there could no longer survive.

Today, Missouri's plants and animals are threatened by species that are new to the state. Many of these new species have no natural predators in Missouri, and they can easily overwhelm the local species. For example, zebra mussels, which are native to Russia, have spread throughout the region. They eat so many of the tiny plants and animals that float in the water that there is nothing left for the native mussels to eat. Silver carp, Asian carp, and rusty crayfish have also invaded Missouri's rivers. They, too, eat so much that they threaten the native fish.

Since 2005, it has been illegal to possess these creatures. The Missouri Conservation Department is working to help Missourians get rid of these species. Missourians who own land on streams and lakes are being encouraged to keep the shorelines clean so that wildlife can move along them without danger. Missouri is determined to protect its natural environment for generations to come.

A diver holds a clam infested with zebra mussels.

READ ABOUT

Prehistoric peoples hunted mammoths with bows and arrows.

c. 12,000 BCE

The first humans enter what is now Missouri

c. 8000 BCE

The Dalton people develop stone knives

▲ **c. 7000 BCE**

Archaic Indian culture develops

FIRST PEOPLE

★

T HE FIRST HUMANS TO ENTER THE REGION THAT BECAME MISSOURI ARRIVED AROUND 12,000 BCE. These people, called Paleo-Indians, hunted mammoths, mastodons, and giant bison. By about 10,000 BCE, Paleo-Indians known as the Ozark Bluff Dwellers lived in caves on bluffs, or cliffs, above rivers. Over time, the climate got warmer, and the ancient animals became extinct. Life was changing in Missouri.

c. 1000 BCE ▶
Woodland culture develops

c. 1000 CE
Mississippians begin building temple mounds

1300
Native American nations begin forming in what is now Missouri

Native American Peoples

(Before European Contact)

This map shows the general area of Native American peoples before European settlers arrived.

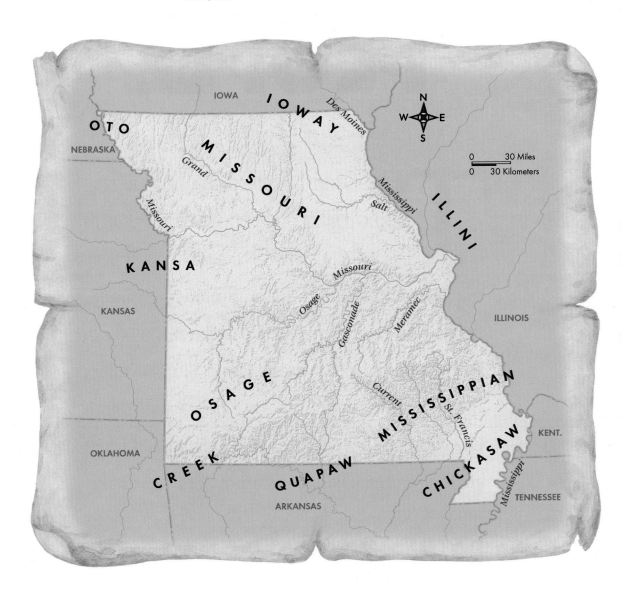

THE ANCIENT PEOPLE

After the giant mammals died out, Paleo-Indians began hunting smaller animals such as deer, squirrels, and raccoons. By perhaps 10,000 years ago, a group of Paleo-Indians called the Dalton people had developed sharp stone knives that they used to cut up deer and other animals. Their stone knives are called Dalton points.

About 9,000 years ago, the Archaic culture developed. The climate was growing warmer and drier, which meant that forests were disappearing. The Archaic Indians developed a weapon called the atlatl, which was useful for hunting in open areas rather than in the woods. An atlatl is a stick that can propel a spear faster and farther than a human arm can.

Woodland culture developed around 3,000 years ago in the eastern part of the continent. Both Paleo-Indians and Archaic people had moved from place to place as seasons changed and game migrated. Woodland people lived a more settled existence. They built round houses of wood, mud, and thatch (reeds and straw). They grew crops and made clay pottery in which they stored water, vegetables, and seeds. They also began to hunt with bows and arrows. Some of the Woodland people, called Hopewell, began to build large mounds of earth.

This Archaic culture knife blade, which dates from 8000 BCE to 6000 BCE, was discovered in Missouri.

FAQ

Q8 WHERE DID THE DALTON PEOPLE GET THEIR NAME?

A8 Their name comes from Sidna Poage Dalton, the chief justice of the Missouri Supreme Court and an amateur **archaeologist**. He found knives at several sites in central Missouri in 1948.

WORD TO KNOW

archaeologist *a person who studies the remains of past human societies*

Woodland pottery

THE MOUND BUILDERS

Around 1,000 years ago, some of the people, especially in the Mississippi valley, began to build large, permanent communities. The towns were clustered around flat-topped mounds, some as tall as 10-story buildings. These people, called Mississippians, probably used the mounds both for ceremonies and as burial grounds. Some religious and political leaders lived on top of the mounds.

The largest Indian mounds north of Mexico are found at Cahokia, Illinois, just across the river from St. Louis. There are almost 70 mounds there. Missouri has its own mounds, also along the Mississippi River. The largest number is in Pemiscot County, in the Bootheel. There were once many more mounds around St. Louis, but they were destroyed as the area became more developed by European settlers.

Mississippian water bottles discovered in Mississippi County, Missouri

This mural shows Mississippian women and children doing chores.

The Mississippian Indians also traded with other groups of people far away. Through this trade, they acquired copper and other goods. In 1906, some ornate and ancient copper plates were found in a Missouri field. The plates were made from copper that came from northern Michigan.

NATIVE AMERICAN NATIONS

By about 1300 CE, Native American nations began to develop. Many different peoples moved through Missouri. In the mound-building area of southeastern Missouri, Creek and Chickasaw societies developed in about 1300. The Quapaw people lived west of the Chickasaw nation, mostly in the area that became Arkansas. The neighboring Illini people (also called Illiniwek) moved back and forth across the Mississippi River in hollowed-out logs.

A Mississippian face embossed in copper

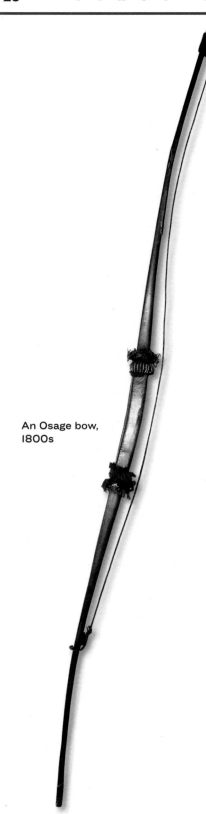

An Osage bow,
1800s

They regarded the territory adjacent to the Mississippi River and north of Quapaw territory as theirs.

The Missouri (or Missouria) people lived in earth-covered domed houses clustered into villages. In the summer, they left their villages to hunt buffalo on the western plains. The Ioway and Oto nations were related people who held small sections of land in what is now northern Missouri.

THE OSAGE PEOPLE

The Osage nation was Missouri's largest Native American group. Osages lived in what is now the southern half of Missouri. The name *Osage* was a French mispronunciation of the group's name, *Wazhazhe*, meaning "upstream people."

Osages believed that they came to earth along the branches of a red oak tree that grew in the lowest of four worlds. Then they split into two groups, the peace people and the war people. The peace people, or Tsishu, took up farming. They were probably related to the Omaha, Ponca, Kansa, and Quapaw peoples. The war people became the Osage nation. They believed that honor stemmed from guarding their land and carrying out acts of war. Because of this, they made frequent raids into neighboring villages. They were a tall, powerful people. Many of the men stood at least 6 feet (183 cm) tall.

Osages lived in villages of longhouses. The longhouses were built of wooden poles covered with woven mats or buffalo skins. Several families lived in each longhouse. Both men and women wore clothing of deerskin.

Osages were great hunters. The men sometimes left the Ozarks to pursue bison on the nearby plains. The women tended crops, such as corn, beans, and pumpkins. They also collected fruits and nuts.

In this George Catlin painting from 1846–48, an Osage hunter pursues a buffalo.

The Osage people seasoned their food with salt. Mineral springs are common on the edges of the Ozarks, where mineral-filled water bubbles up through the limestone. As the water evaporates, salt is left behind in dried piles. These piles are called salt licks, because animals visit them to lick the salt. Osages also came to the salt licks to acquire salt.

Soon, new people would come to Missouri in search of salt, animal skins, and land. They would gradually push out the Native Americans who had long called the area home.

READ ABOUT

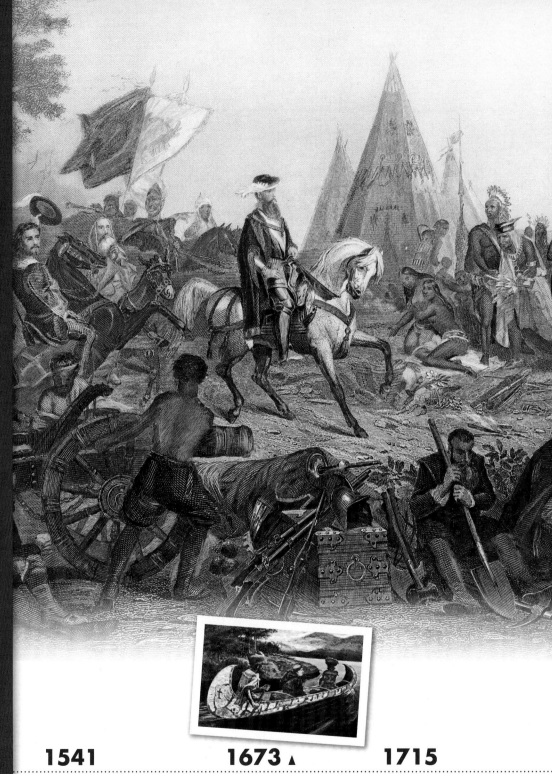

Hernando de Soto
near the Mississippi
River in 1541

1541

Hernando de Soto and
his party become the first
Europeans to enter what
is now Missouri

1673 ▲

Jacques Marquette
and Louis Jolliet begin
exploring the Mississippi
River

1715

Slaves are brought into
Missouri to mine lead

CHAPTER THREE

EXPLORATION AND SETTLEMENT

★

I N 1539, SPANISH EXPLORER HERNANDO DE SOTO ARRIVED IN WHAT IS NOW FLORIDA WITH A FLEET OF 10 SHIPS. He was searching for gold. In 1541, de Soto's continued search for riches brought him and his men into what is now southeastern Missouri. De Soto, who never found the gold he sought, died soon after, and the leaderless expedition headed to Mexico. Europeans did not return to Missouri for more than a century.

1735

Ste. Genevieve becomes the first permanent European settlement in Missouri

1803 ▶

The United States buys Louisiana Territory, which includes Missouri

1820

Congress creates the Missouri Compromise

European Exploration of Missouri

The colored arrows on this map show the routes taken by explorers between 1673 and 1807.

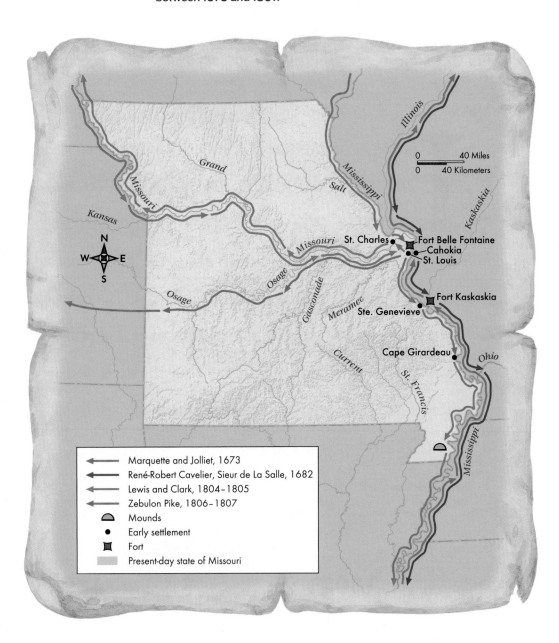

Marquette and Jolliet, 1673
René-Robert Cavelier, Sieur de La Salle, 1682
Lewis and Clark, 1804–1805
Zebulon Pike, 1806–1807
Mounds
Early settlement
Fort
Present-day state of Missouri

Jacques Marquette, Louis Jolliet, and an American Indian guide exploring the Mississippi River

THE FRENCH ARRIVE

In 1673, the French in Canada sent a priest, Father Jacques Marquette, and a young adventurer, Louis Jolliet, to explore the Mississippi valley. They traveled in canoes all the way to Missouri before returning home. A few years later, in 1682, explorer René-Robert Cavelier, Sieur de La Salle, traveled all the way down the Mississippi to the mouth of the river. He claimed the entire Mississippi River valley for France. He named it Louisiana, after the French king Louis XIV.

European traders and **missionaries** soon moved into the area. The region's first-known European resident was a French priest, Father Gabriel Marest. He lived with members of the Kaskaskia nation on the west bank of the Mississippi River. Traders joined them, but they failed to build a permanent village.

WORD TO KNOW

missionaries *people who try to convert others to a religion*

Soon, other Frenchmen arrived to mine lead. At the time, lead was used to make bullets, pipes, weights, and many other objects. The first lead mine in Missouri was located at Mine La Motte, near Fredericktown in the southeast. Frenchmen began digging there in 1715. They brought enslaved African people to work in the mines. This was the start of African enslavement in Missouri.

NATIVE AMERICAN NEWCOMERS

Native Americans from the East also came through the area. British colonists on the Atlantic coast had been taking land from various Native American groups since they had founded Virginia in 1607. Some Cherokees began to leave their traditional lands in the Southeast in the hope of finding peace. As early as 1721, Cherokees began settling in southeastern Missouri. They became known as the Lost Cherokee. Some Delawares, who traditionally lived on the mid-Atlantic coast, also searched for peace in the West. Some settled in the southwestern part of Missouri.

THE FRENCH SETTLE IN

The Spanish thought they should control the Mississippi valley as a result of de Soto's journey. To prevent the Spanish from claiming the Missouri region, the French sent explorer Étienne Véniard de Bourgmond to build a colony there. In 1723, he built Fort Orleans in northern Missouri, near where the Grand and Missouri rivers meet. But by 1728, the fort had disappeared.

In 1735, the French finally managed to establish a permanent settlement. The town of Ste. Genevieve was founded by French people who moved across the Mississippi River from Illinois. This new town had salt springs and lead mines.

The French community of Ste. Genevieve established a school for poor children, both European and Native American, as early as 1806.

The second permanent European settlement in Missouri was not established until 1764. That year, the French governor of Louisiana sent Pierre Laclède to establish a fur-trading post where the Mississippi and Missouri rivers met. Laclède called his post St. Louis. It quickly became an important location for both French settlers and Native Americans. At St. Louis, Indians would trade their furs for tobacco, muskets, and cloth. Laclède and others, concerned that the American Indians might not produce enough furs to meet their demands, began to employ hunters and trappers. Soon, a large portion of St. Louis's economy depended on furs.

SPANISH CONTROL

In 1754, the French and Indian War began. In this war, the French and the British were battling for control of the continent and the fur trade. By 1762, the French were losing badly. France **ceded** its land west of the Mississippi to its ally Spain so that Britain would not claim it at the war's end.

WOW

In 2014, St. Louis celebrated its 250th birthday with a variety of cultural events and exhibits.

WORD TO KNOW

ceded *gave up or granted*

Pierre Laclède established a post at what would become the city of St. Louis.

DANIEL BOONE: TRAILBLAZER

Daniel Boone (1734–1820) was born in a frontier settlement in Pennsylvania. He became a soldier, hunter, and explorer. In 1775, he led a group that blazed a trail through the Cumberland Gap in the Appalachian Mountains. He established the town of Boonesborough, Kentucky. In 1799, he headed west again, this time to Missouri. The Spanish hired Boone to keep law and order and paid him with land in Missouri. He lost the land, however, when the United States bought the Louisiana Territory. He died in Missouri.

Want to know more? Visit www.factsfornow.scholastic.com and enter the keyword **Missouri**.

Between 1775 and 1810, about 300,000 settlers headed west through the Cumberland Gap, which was opened by Daniel Boone.

In 1775, the British became involved in another war when the British colonies on the East Coast began a fight for their independence. Many French and Spanish settlers in the Missouri region supported the Americans against the British. Some helped American troops. Because of this, the British and their Native American allies launched an attack on St. Louis in 1780, but the people of St. Louis, under the command of Captain Fernando de Leyba, repelled the attack. By 1783, the American colonists had won the war. The East Coast was now part of a new nation, but Missouri remained in Spanish hands.

During colonial times, few Americans ventured west of the Appalachian Mountains, a long mountain range that separates the eastern seaboard from the rest of the continent. There was no easy way to get across the mountains. But then, in 1775, an explorer and soldier named Daniel Boone blazed a trail through the Cumberland Gap, a low spot in the mountains. The trail was soon widened to become an important part of the Wilderness Road, which allowed settlers to quickly spread west of the Appalachian Mountains.

Many settlers continued across the Mississippi River into Spanish Louisiana because the Spanish allowed enslavement. Slavery was banned in some of the American territory east of the river.

By 1800, Spain was busy fighting a war in Europe. The Spanish had lost interest in their North American land, so they traded the Louisiana Territory, including Missouri, back to the French.

THE LOUISIANA PURCHASE

The French also soon lost interest in Louisiana. In 1803, President Thomas Jefferson offered to buy the whole of Louisiana Territory, paying the French about $23 million. The Louisiana Purchase turned out to be one of the greatest deals in history. Some or all of 15 states would eventually be created out of the roughly 830,000 square miles (2.1 million sq km) between the Mississippi River and the Rocky Mountains. It cost just over four cents an acre.

The region's transition to U.S. control was far from smooth. People fought over the issue of enslavement, land titles, and mine stakes. These conflicts sometimes became violent.

Just what had Jefferson purchased? He wanted to know more about this vast land that was now part of the United States. Jefferson asked his personal secretary, Meriwether Lewis, to lead an expedition to explore the Louisiana Purchase. Lewis asked an old army friend, William Clark, to join him. Clark agreed, adding that York, an enslaved man who had served Clark for many years, would also go along. They hired more than 40 other people to join their Corps of Discovery.

In May 1804, the Corps of Discovery left St. Louis heading up the Missouri River. It would be more than two years before they returned. During that time,

The Louisiana Purchase nearly doubled the size of the United States in 1803.

Louisiana Purchase

This map shows the area (in yellow) that made up the Louisiana Purchase and the present-day state of Missouri (in orange).

STEAMBOATS ON THE RIVERS

People began using the power of steam to drive boats in 1807. The steam turned big paddles, which pushed against the water, moving the boat. Within a few years, steamboats were carrying passengers and freight along the Mississippi River at the amazing speed of 8 miles (13 km) per hour going downstream and 3 miles (5 km) per hour upstream.

The first steamboats traveled up the Mississippi to St. Louis in 1817. By 1819, they were also moving along the Missouri River. They soon became the major means of carrying cargo in Missouri. In 1860, more than 3,000 steamboats docked in St. Louis. Steamboats remained the primary means of travel on the rivers even after railroads were built in the 1850s and 1860s. They finally disappeared in the early 20th century, as their costs increased and railroads cut their prices.

A view of St. Louis in 1832

they journeyed all the way to the Pacific Ocean. They met members of almost 50 different Native American nations. They discovered 300 kinds of plants and animals that no European had seen before, from prairie dogs to porcupines. And they mapped much of the land. They also claimed the Pacific Northwest for the United States.

GROWING SETTLEMENTS

St. Louis was small when Lewis and Clark began their exploration. The first steamboats arrived in St. Louis in 1817, bringing more people. Many people planned to go west, but some stayed in St. Louis, providing goods and services to the people who followed them. Gradually, a great city developed.

Settlement in the Ozarks was limited for a time because the first steamboats could not travel on the winding rivers that ran through the region. Finally, smaller, more maneuverable steamboats were built. Once the ship captains learned to navigate Ozark rivers such as the Gasconade and the Osage, a new part of Missouri was opened to white settlement.

Many of the first white settlers in the Ozarks had moved there from the Appalachians. They lived by hunting and fishing. Eventually, the supply of natural food diminished, and they tried farming instead. The land was not very fertile, however. Most people could produce enough crops to feed their families but little more.

NATIVE AMERICANS ON THE MOVE

Meanwhile, Osages continued to live and hunt in the Ozarks, as they had for generations. Osages sometimes raided early French settlements in the area. But they soon learned that they could benefit if they traded with the French. Osages

Native Americans trading furs for weapons and other goods

traded furs for guns, and for a time, the Osage people prospered. But as more Europeans moved into the area, Osages were pushed off their land.

Other Native American groups were also moving into Missouri. In the late 18th century, some Delawares had moved south from Ohio and settled on the Gasconade River near Cape Girardeau. Sauks and Mesquakies came into Missouri from the Great Lakes region. They had been pushed out both by the French and by the Iroquois people from farther east.

Most Native groups in what is now Missouri had supported the British during the American Revolution and the War of 1812. When that war ended in 1815, the U.S. government forced these Native Americans to give up their lands. By 1816, many Native Americans had been removed to areas west and south of Missouri Territory.

BECOMING A STATE

Year by year, more and more European Americans moved into Missouri Territory. By 1818, Missouri had a large enough population to become a state. But not all Americans wanted Missouri to be a state.

At the time, the United States was made up of an equal number of Slave States and Free States. Enslavement was legal in Missouri. Some people in Congress did not want Missouri to become a state unless another state that outlawed slavery entered the Union at the same time. They wanted to retain the balance between Slave and Free States.

Finally, in 1820, Congress came up with the Missouri Compromise, which allowed Missouri to enter the Union as a Slave State at the same time that Maine was admitted as a Free State. In the agreement, Congress set Missouri's southern border at 36°30' north **latitude**. The compromise also stated that any other states formed from the

MISSOURI ADDS THE BOOTHEEL

A rancher named John Hardeman Walker owned most of the Bootheel. When Missourians petitioned to become a state in 1818, the first plan left Walker's land out of the state. But he wanted to be under Missouri's laws, not those of Arkansas, which wasn't yet eligible for statehood. Congress agreed to Walker's request, and the Bootheel also became part of Missouri.

WORD TO KNOW

latitude *the position of a place, measured in degrees north or south of the equator*

Missouri: From Territory to Statehood

(1812–1821)

This map shows the original Missouri Territory and the area that became the state of Missouri in 1821.

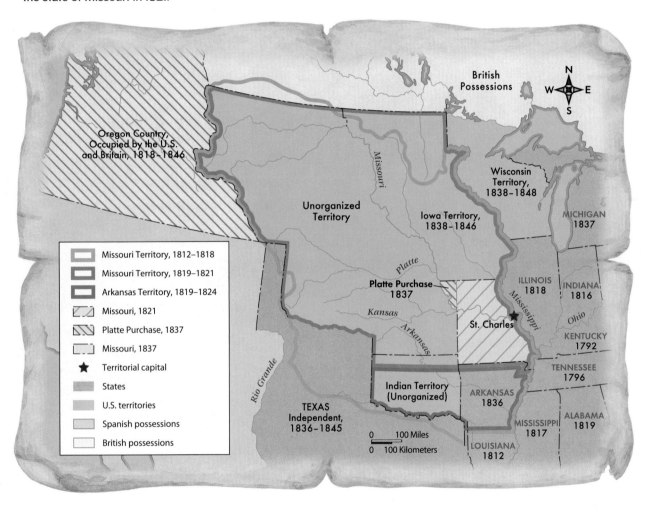

Legend:
- Missouri Territory, 1812–1818
- Missouri Territory, 1819–1821
- Arkansas Territory, 1819–1824
- Missouri, 1821
- Platte Purchase, 1837
- Missouri, 1837
- ★ Territorial capital
- States
- U.S. territories
- Spanish possessions
- British possessions

Map labels:
British Possessions

Oregon Country, Occupied by the U.S. and Britain, 1818–1846

Unorganized Territory

Wisconsin Territory, 1838–1848

Iowa Territory, 1838–1846

MICHIGAN 1837

Missouri

Platte

Platte Purchase 1837

ILLINOIS 1818

INDIANA 1816

Kansas

Mississippi

Ohio

St. Charles

KENTUCKY 1792

Arkansas

TENNESSEE 1796

Rio Grande

Indian Territory (Unorganized)

ARKANSAS 1836

TEXAS Independent, 1836–1845

0   100 Miles
0   100 Kilometers

MISSISSIPPI 1817

ALABAMA 1819

LOUISIANA 1812

Louisiana Purchase north of Missouri's southern border would be Free States. The Missouri Compromise settled the issue of enslavement in the territories for a time, but the question would come back to haunt Missouri—and the entire United States.

42

READ ABOUT

A scene from the
last slave auction
in St. Louis, 1865

1821▲

*Missouri becomes
the 24th state*

1836

*Native Americans are forced to
leave northwestern Missouri to
prepare for the Platte Purchase*

1843

*Pioneers begin leaving
Missouri along the
Oregon Trail*

CHAPTER FOUR

GROWTH AND CHANGE

★

MISSOURI WAS ADMITTED TO THE UNION ON AUGUST 10, 1821, AS A STATE IN WHICH SLAVERY WAS LEGAL. Its central location in the United States would soon put it in the middle of the struggle over enslavement. But it would also be the frontier, the starting place for adventures.

1857 ▲

The Supreme Court rules that enslaved Missourian Dred Scott has no right to sue for his freedom

1860

The Pony Express is established to carry mail from Missouri to California

1865 ►

Missouri becomes the first slaveholding state to end slavery

Cherokees fighting the cold on the Trail of Tears in 1838

SEE IT HERE!

TRAIL OF TEARS STATE PARK

Trail of Tears State Park at Jackson is located where nine of 13 groups of Cherokees traveling the Trail of Tears crossed the Mississippi River. Winter had set in, and they had to camp on the site until the weather improved. Dozens died before they could cross the river. The park is part of the Trail of Tears National Historic Trail, a memorial to all the Indians who died along their forced journey to Indian Territory.

NATIVE AMERICAN REMOVAL

The population of the United States was growing quickly around the time Missouri became a state. Americans in the East wanted more land. In response, President Andrew Jackson signed the Indian Removal Act of 1830. This act forced Native Americans in the East to give up their land and move to Indian Territory in what is now Oklahoma.

The Cherokee nation was the largest Native American landholder in the East. Cherokees fought their removal by every means possible, but in the end, they lost. In 1838, the U.S. Army forced them on a 1,200-mile (1,900 km) journey west that is known as the Trail of Tears. For many, the trip was a death march. About one-fourth of the 15,000 Indians died along the way from hunger, cold, and disease. One of two main routes of the Trail of Tears passed through southern Missouri.

In the meantime, the Sauk and Mesquakie people from Wisconsin had been forced into the Platte River region of northwestern Missouri. The United States also moved several other Native groups into that area. White settlers were supposed to keep out of the region, but they didn't. They wanted the land.

In 1836, President Andrew Jackson forced the Native people of the Platte Purchase area to give up their land. When completed the next year, the purchase added an area the size of Rhode Island and Delaware combined to the northwestern corner of Missouri. The Native Americans who lived there were soon moved to Kansas.

In 1838, the Missouri legislature passed a law making it illegal for Native Americans to live in Missouri. Rather than be forced into Indian Territory, many Native Americans gave up their traditional ways and tried to blend in with white society. Missouri did not enforce the law in later years, but it was not officially **repealed** until 1909.

NEW COMMUNITIES

In 1831, Joseph Smith, the founder of the Church of Jesus Christ of Latter-day Saints (also called the Mormons), declared western Missouri the new home for his followers. There they would be able to live in peace. The Mormons

MINI-BIO

ALEXANDER McNAIR: FIRST GOVERNOR

Missouri's first governor, Alexander McNair (1775–1826) was born in Pennsylvania. He settled in St. Louis in 1804. McNair served in many posts before becoming governor, including sheriff of St. Louis County and U.S. marshal of the Missouri Territory. He was also a member of the territory's constitutional convention. In 1820, McNair was elected governor and served until 1824. He then served as an agent for the Osage people until his death.

❓ **Want to know more?** Visit www.factsfornow .scholastic.com and enter the keyword **Missouri**.

WORD TO KNOW

repealed *withdrawn; canceled*

believed that Jesus Christ would return to Earth both in Jerusalem and in Independence, Missouri.

Differences between the Mormons and their non-Mormon neighbors started almost immediately. Mormons tended to keep to themselves, and they also tended to vote for Mormon candidates. Non-Mormons feared that they would take control of western Missouri. Non-Mormons drove the Mormons first out of Jackson County and then out of Clay County. The Missouri government created Caldwell County in 1836 specifically for the Mormons. But several skirmishes followed in what is called the Mormon War. Because of the fighting, Governor Lilburn W. Boggs expelled the Mormons from Missouri entirely. His order read that the Mormons "must be exterminated or driven from the state." The Mormons settled first in Illinois before heading farther west and founding present-day Utah.

Other new communities also flourished in Missouri. In 1824, Gottfried Duden came to Missouri to look into helping other Germans immigrate. The book he wrote described Missouri in glorious terms. He said he found "beautiful nature for hundreds of miles—hills and valleys covered with trees as if an artist had created a park—your choice of climates—cheap and fertile lands." Thousands of Germans followed him to that seemingly enchanted place, founding towns such as Hermann in central Missouri. Today, descendents of German immigrants remain the largest ethnic group in the state.

WAGON TRAINS WEST!

When the United States took over the Louisiana Territory, Spain still ruled Mexico. Spain did not allow other countries to trade with Mexico, which at the time included the areas that are now Arizona, New Mexico, and Texas. In 1821, Mexico won its independence from Spain, and the newly

Ann Hawkins Gentry was an early settler in the city of Columbia, Missouri. In 1838, she became Columbia's postmistress, a position she held until 1865. She was the second female postmaster in the country.

The town of Independence, about 1850

independent Mexicans were eager for American goods. William Becknell, a trader from Franklin, Missouri, soon rolled into Santa Fe with a wagonload of goods.

He was soon traveling back and forth, leading wagon trains to Santa Fe. The route he followed became the Santa Fe Trail. Traders brought fabric, mirrors, and iron goods to Santa Fe and returned with furs, horses, and mules. In 1827, the town of Franklin was washed away when the Missouri River flooded. The new town of Independence was built as far west as steamboats could carry goods on the Missouri River. Enslaved Africans built most of Independence. It became the head of the Santa Fe Trail.

The Oregon Trail also started in Independence. Pioneers followed this trail west to start new lives in the

W★W

On May 17, 1849, most of downtown St. Louis, along with 23 steamboats docked on the river, were destroyed by fire.

FAQ

Q8 WHEN WAS KANSAS CITY FOUNDED?

A8 In 1821, Frenchman François Chouteau founded a fur-trading post where the Missouri and the Kansas rivers join. The trading post was destroyed by flood, but in 1833, J. C. McCoy founded the town of Westport at that same location. During the next decade, a town called Kansas was also founded in the area. In 1889, the city of Kansas became Kansas City, and in 1897, Westport became part of that city.

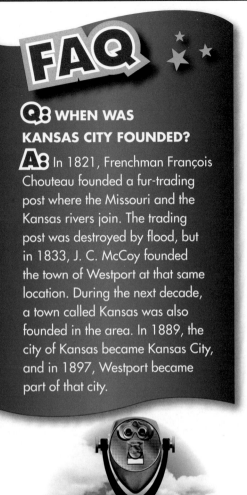

SEE IT HERE!

MISSOURI TOWN

Many people moved west from Missouri, but many people also stayed. You can see how they lived at Missouri Town 1855, located in Lee's Summit, near Kansas City. Many historic buildings, including log cabins, a tavern, and a schoolhouse, have been moved to one site. The town is so realistic that several films have been shot there.

Oregon Country. The pioneers would gather outside Independence in April. Then they waited for the grass to grow. It had to be tall enough for their oxen or mules to graze along the route. Large numbers of pioneers first traveled the trail in 1843. In the next 25 years, thousands of pioneers would make the journey.

After gold was discovered in California in 1848, other Missouri cities began competing with Independence as a jumping-off point for people heading west. Westport (which became Kansas City) and St. Joseph both boomed in the 1850s. Missouri businesspeople provided the pioneers everything they needed to travel west. They built covered wagons, they raised and sold oxen to pull the wagons, and they sold the travelers supplies for the journey, often at outrageous prices.

In the 1830s, railroad companies had begun laying track in the eastern United States. By the 1850s, railroads crisscrossed the East. The first railroad to cross Missouri was completed in 1859, but no lines crossed the Great Plains. This meant there was no easy way to get mail from the East Coast to the West Coast. Some letters destined for California were put on boats that traveled all the way around the southern tip of South America. It took months for the letters to arrive. In 1857, Congress awarded John Butterfield's stagecoach company a contract to carry mail across the continent. Butterfield's stagecoaches picked up the mail from Tipton, in central Missouri. This was the railroad's westernmost station. Butterfield could get the mail to San Francisco, California, in 25 days. In Missouri alone he had several relay stations where horses were changed. They were usually about 20 miles (32 km) apart.

Soon, the Pony Express was established to provide even faster mail service. On April 30, 1860, a lone rider set out from St. Joseph, Missouri, carrying U.S. mail in his

The first Pony Express rider setting out from St. Joseph in 1860

saddlebags. During the coming days, that mail was transferred between 80 riders who used 420 horses stationed at 190 relay stations. The mail arrived in Sacramento, California, in just 10 days.

The Pony Express lasted only 16 months. In 1861, workers finished stringing cables for the first **transcontinental** telegraph. Now Americans with urgent messages could easily wire telegrams. Then in 1869, workers hammered in the final spike on the first railway to connect the East Coast and the West Coast. Railroads were now the fastest and easiest way to deliver mail across the continent.

WORD TO KNOW

transcontinental *crossing an entire continent*

Blanche Kelso Bruce

The first African American to serve a full term in the U.S. Senate was Blanche Kelso Bruce, who spent most of his youth in Missouri. After the Civil War, he became a wealthy farmer, and in 1874, Mississippi elected him to the U.S. Senate.

SLAVERY AND EDUCATION

After Missouri entered the Union, slaveholders from Kentucky and Tennessee became the new state's ruling class. As slaveholders became entrenched in the government, the legislature passed laws called slave codes that denied enslaved people any right to an education and tried to prevent free people of color from moving to the state.

Nuns at the St. Louis Catholic Cathedral violated the law against teaching enslaved people to read and write. They ran a secret school for enslaved people. One of their graduates, James M. Turner, went on to attend Oberlin College, a top school in Ohio. After the Civil War, he taught in Missouri's first public school for African Americans and was a founder of Lincoln University in Jefferson City. He eventually was appointed state superintendent of Missouri schools for African Americans.

Also violating the 1847 education law was John B. Meachum, an enslaved Virginian who purchased his freedom and moved to Missouri around 1821. Ordained as a Baptist minister, Meachum founded the First African Baptist Church of St. Louis, the first black Protestant church west of the Mississippi. He regularly helped black children learn to read and write.

TENSIONS GROW

Southerners were determined to preserve enslavement in order to keep their huge profitable plantations running. Most Missouri farms were small, however, and few Missouri farmers owned more than one or two slaves. Missourians in cities worked mainly in factories and other businesses. They did not own enslaved people. As a result, opinions on the issues of slavery were divided between rural and urban Missourians.

Some Missourians moved to Kansas Territory to help turn it into a Slave State.

In 1854, Congress passed the Kansas-Nebraska Act. It replaced the Missouri Compromise, which banned slavery in Northern territories and allowed it in Southern territories. The Kansas-Nebraska Act instead gave each territory the right to decide for itself whether to allow slavery.

Many Missourians wanted the neighboring Kansas Territory to become a Slave State. Some even moved there so they could vote in favor of it becoming a Slave State. Others didn't move to Kansas, but simply crossed the border to vote, daring election officials to stop them. In 1856, a few well-armed Missourians went to the town of Lawrence, Kansas, and burned a hotel that was the center of the antislavery movement. Kansans responded by sending raiders into Missouri. The border conflict became known as Bleeding Kansas.

THE DRED SCOTT CASE

The most important slave case in American history began in St. Louis. Dred Scott had been born into slavery. In the 1830s, his master took him to Illinois and Minnesota, neither of which allowed slavery. Scott and his master returned to St. Louis in 1842. In 1846, with encouragement from his wife, Harriet, Scott filed a lawsuit in St. Louis arguing that because he had lived in places where slavery was banned, he should be freed. Scott's legal battle lasted 11 years. Finally, in 1857, the U.S. Supreme Court ruled against him. Chief Justice Roger Taney, a Maryland slaveholder, wrote the decision. The Court said that people of African descent could not be U.S. citizens, and as a noncitizen, Scott had no right to file a lawsuit. The Court also said that the federal government did not have the power to ban slavery in the territories. Although he lost in court, abolitionists soon bought Dred and Harriet Scott. They were freed within a year, inflaming passions on both sides of the slavery debate.

Dred Scott

WOW

Only two counties in the entire South voted for Abraham Lincoln in the 1860 election, and both of them were in Missouri.

WORD TO KNOW

abolitionists *people who worked to end slavery*

The following year, the U.S. Supreme Court ruled in the case of Dred Scott, an enslaved man in St. Louis who had sued for his freedom. In its decision, the Court stated that the Missouri Compromise was not legal under the U.S. Constitution and the United States had no right to ban slavery in territories. The decision infuriated **abolitionists**.

In 1860, Abraham Lincoln was elected president. Many Southerners were convinced that Lincoln would end slavery. Not long after his election, Southern states began to secede, or withdraw, from the United States. They formed a new nation, the Confederate States of America. Lincoln was willing to fight to stop the nation from breaking apart. The country was on the verge of civil war.

MISSOURI IN THE CIVIL WAR

In Missouri, the legislature voted to hold a special convention to decide whether the state should secede. The delegates to the convention decided that Missouri should remain neutral in the war.

But Missouri governor Claiborne Jackson favored seceding. He was prepared to do all he could to swing Missouri over to the South's side. When President Lincoln called up four regiments of Missouri soldiers to fight for the Union, the governor refused to cooperate.

In May 1861, Jackson prepared his state military units to attack the St. Louis **Arsenal**. Nathaniel Lyon, the arsenal's commander, supported the Union. His own troops soon surrounded Jackson's soldiers and forced them to surrender. Lyon captured the capital and put a pro-Union government in place.

The first big Civil War battle in Missouri took place on August 10 near Wilson's Creek in the southwestern part of the state. Lyon was killed. He was the first general to die in the Civil War. The Confederates won the Battle of Wilson's Creek and took control of nearby Springfield. But Missouri as a whole remained under Union control. The pro-Confederate government moved to Neosho in October and set up its own legislature, which voted to

The death of General Nathaniel Lyon at the Battle of Wilson's Creek

WORD TO KNOW

arsenal *a place where weapons are made or stored*

WOW

During the Civil War, the U.S. Navy hired St. Louis engineer James Eads to quickly build ironclad ships—wood-framed ships covered in iron. Eads built seven ironclad ships in fewer than 100 days.

WORD TO KNOW

guerrilla *describing soldiers who don't belong to regular armies; they often use surprise attacks and other uncommon battle tactics*

secede. The Missouri Confederates later fled Neosho for Texas. Meanwhile, Hamilton R. Gamble became the acting governor of Missouri. Through his efforts, Missouri stayed in the Union.

Early in the war, the Union cut the Confederacy in half by taking control of the Mississippi River. General Ulysses S. Grant led this effort. He would later command the entire Union army.

Later in the war, **guerrilla** raids were common in Missouri. Small bands of raiders attacked any military location they could find. Some Kansans raided Missouri, stealing slaveholders' horses and cattle and driving them into Kansas to be sold. These raiders were called Jayhawkers.

Missouri Confederate raider William Quantrill brought terror to the hearts of many. A number of teenage Missourians joined his band, including brothers named Frank and Jesse James.

To try to stop the violence, Union general Thomas Ewing arrested the wives, mothers, and sisters of known raiders. When several of the women were accidentally killed, Quantrill and his men burned Lawrence, Kansas, and killed at least 150 men and boys. Ewing responded by trying to clear the border of all pro-Confederate settlers. Their homes and crops were burned.

MINI-BIO

SPOTSWOOD RICE: ESCAPE TO FREEDOM

Spotswood Rice (ca. 1824–?) was born into slavery in Virginia. After years of abuse on a Missouri tobacco plantation, he ran away and found freedom with the Union army during the Civil War. In 1864, he enlisted in a regiment of the U.S. Colored Infantry and served as a military nurse. While in service, Rice wrote letters back to his family to reassure them that they would all soon be reunited. He was right. By 1880, Rice and his wife and children were all living together in St. Louis. Rice's letters show the hardships enslaved people faced trying to keep their families together.

❓ Want to know more? Visit www.factsfornow .scholastic.com and enter the keyword **Missouri**.

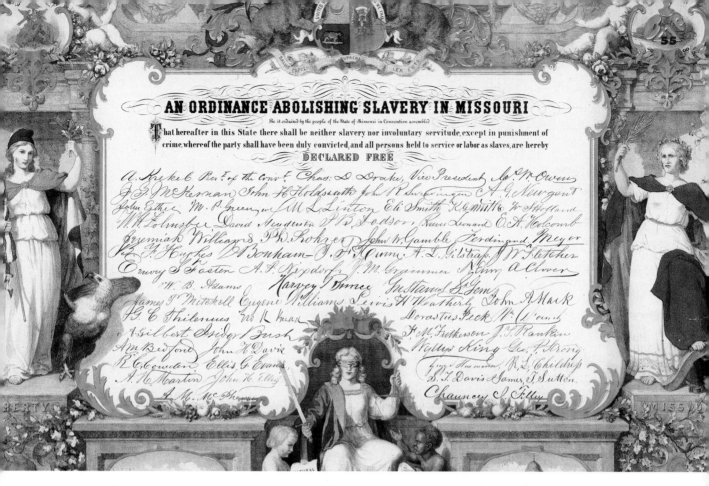

AN ORDINANCE ABOLISHING SLAVERY IN MISSOURI

Be it ordained by the people of the State of Missouri in Convention assembled

That hereafter in this State there shall be neither slavery nor involuntary servitude, except in punishment of crime, whereof the party shall have been duly convicted, and all persons held to service or labor as slaves, are hereby

DECLARED FREE

This document officially ended slavery in Missouri in 1865.

The war provided Missouri's enslaved men, women, and children a chance to break their chains, and many did. A young slave named Robert Hickman organized dozens of other enslaved men, women, and children to make a bold strike for freedom. They built a large raft near the Missouri River and took their families aboard. They headed east to the Mississippi and then north to freedom.

By 1864, about 24,000 enslaved people in Missouri had fled their owners and found liberty. About 8,400 former Missouri slaves fought in the Civil War.

Missouri formally ended slavery on January 11, 1865. It was the first slaveholding state to do so. The Union won the Civil War three months later. And by the end of 1865, the 13th Amendment to the U.S. Constitution abolished slavery across the nation.

About 186,000 people of color served in the Union army and helped end slavery and preserve the Union.

MINI-BIO

CALAMITY JANE: WILD WEST HEROINE

Calamity Jane, one of the most colorful characters of the Wild West, was born Martha Jane Cannary (1852–1903) on a farm near Princeton, Missouri. She had no schooling, but she grew up to become a great horse rider and rifle shot. In 1870, she became an army scout, and she later fought with U.S. troops against Native Americans. After traveling the West for many years, she began to appear in Wild West shows as a trick shooter. She was billed as the "heroine of a thousand thrilling adventures." She also wrote her autobiography, but there's no way of telling what parts of it were true.

❓ Want to know more? Visit www.factsfornow .scholastic.com and enter the keyword **Missouri**.

REBUILDING

The raids during the Civil War had taken their toll on Missouri's farms, railroads, industries, and people. After the war, there was much to repair, buildings and relationships alike.

Missouri residents who had been enemies during the war, now had to figure out a way to work together to rebuild the state. At first, the former foes didn't work together. Some Unionists in Missouri who were in positions of power in the government at the end of the war wanted to keep former Confederate supporters out of the state government. These Unionists didn't allow some former Confederates to vote or hold public office, or to work as teachers, lawyers, or ministers. These laws were soon overturned, but the mistrust and anger between Unionists and Confederates continued for many years.

BRIDGES TO THE FUTURE

Missouri's population and economy grew quickly in the years after the Civil War. Between 1860 and 1890, the state's population more than doubled. This growth was helped along by the expansion of the railroads.

In 1869, work was completed on the Hannibal Bridge. The first bridge across the Missouri River, it brought the railroad to Kansas City. The Kansas City Stockyards soon opened. Cattlemen in the West could now ship their cattle

The St. Louis Bridge, crossing the
Mississippi River, opened in 1874.

to Kansas City to be sold to the highest bidder. Previously, they had to sell the cattle to the railroads, taking whatever was offered. Meatpacking became a huge industry in Kansas City, and the city boomed.

It took even longer for a bridge to be built across the Mississippi River to St. Louis. The river water there is as deep as 50 feet (15 m) and sits atop a thick layer of mud. But the people of St. Louis were determined to get a bridge that could carry a railroad to their city. James Eads, a self-taught engineer who had built ironclad ships for the Union army during the Civil War, began working on the problem. He designed three steel arches that reached all the way to the bedrock beneath the mud. Eads's steel bridge—the first ever built—measured 6,442 feet (1,964 m) long. The bridge opened in 1874. St. Louis was now connected to the eastern half of the country by railroad. It was ready to once again become a central transportation hub, as it had been when French settlers chose the city's location more than 100 years earlier.

READ ABOUT

Crowds heading toward Festival Hall during the 1904 world's fair

1904
St. Louis hosts a world's fair

▲ **1931**
The Lake of the Ozarks is created by Bagnell Dam

1941
The United States enters World War II

MORE MODERN TIMES

★

S T. LOUIS HOSTED A HUGE WORLD'S FAIR, THE LOUISIANA PURCHASE EXPOSITION, TO CELEBRATE THE 100TH ANNIVERSARY OF THE LOUISIANA PURCHASE. Millions of people saw exhibits from 45 nations. Many exhibits highlighted new technologies and advancing knowledge. The people of St. Louis had shown the world that they lived in a dynamic city that embraced the future.

1945

President Harry Truman orders atomic bombs dropped on two Japanese cities

1968 ▶

William Clay is elected Missouri's first African American U.S. representative

2011

A tornado strikes Joplin, killing 158 people and injuring about 1,150

Workers moving barrels along a levee in St. Louis

St. Louis hosted the Olympic Games at the time of the world's fair in 1904. It was the first time the Olympics were held in the United States.

WORD TO KNOW

levees *ridges of land built up along a riverbank to prevent flooding*

NEW LAND FOR FARMERS

At the dawn of the 20th century, Missouri was eager to use technology and know-how to improve the lives of its citizens. At that time, most of southeastern Missouri was swampland, which was often flooded by the Mississippi and smaller rivers. The counties in the region combined forces to drain the land permanently and make it productive. They built a huge system of channels to collect and drain the water off the land. Altogether, more than 840 miles (1,400 km) of ditches and 240 miles (380 km) of **levees** were built. More than a million acres of wetlands were turned into farmland.

WORLD WAR I

In 1917, the United States joined its European allies in fighting World War I. The military looked to Missouri for mules, which were used to pull cannons. Mules had been a mainstay of Missouri's economy since the days of the Santa Fe Trail. World War I also created a great demand for lead from Missouri, which was used for ammunition.

WOMEN'S RIGHTS

In the late 19th and early 20th centuries, women brought about many changes. For instance, as early as 1867, some women in Missouri began seeking the right to vote. Virginia Minor of St. Louis tried to register to vote in 1872 but was refused. She

JOHN PERSHING: GENERAL OF THE ARMIES

General John J. Pershing (1860–1948) was born in Laclede. As a young man, he taught in a school for African Americans and then enrolled in the U.S. Military Academy at West Point. He served with distinction in the Spanish-American War of 1898, and by 1906, he had risen to the rank of general. In World War I, he commanded all U.S. military forces. When the United States entered the war in 1917, its French and British allies, who had already been fighting for three years, wanted to divide the U.S. troops among their own units. Pershing insisted that the U.S. troops must fight together. At the war's end, Pershing was given credit for the American success in the war. He was soon promoted to the rank of General of the Armies, a rank created especially for him.

? Want to know more? Visit www.factsfornow .scholastic.com and enter the keyword **Missouri**.

The St. Louis League of Women Voters' office in the 1920s

Remember - Remember
THE 23rd. OF SEPTEMBER
NO. REPRESENTATIO
WITHOUT REGISTRATI

CARRY NATION: BARROOM SMASHER

Carry Nation (1846–1911) was born in Kentucky but raised primarily in Missouri. Her first husband was an alcoholic, fueling her hatred of alcohol. She later came to believe that God had called her to fight against drinking alcohol. After moving to Medicine Lodge, Kansas, where the laws banning alcohol were not enforced, she demanded that the authorities close the saloons. When they paid no attention, she stood in front of them singing religious songs. By 1900, she had succeeded in closing all of Medicine Lodge's saloons. Nation moved on to other towns, first using bricks, and then a hatchet, to break up the places where men drank. In all, she was arrested 30 times.

? Want to know more? Visit www.factsfornow .scholastic.com and enter the keyword **Missouri**.

WORD TO KNOW

temperance *moderation, especially in drinking alcoholic beverages*

Nellie Tayloe Ross, the first woman to be elected governor of a state, was born in Andrew County, Missouri, in 1876. She served as governor of Wyoming from 1925 to 1927.

took her case all the way to the Supreme Court but lost. Minor did not live to see her dream fulfilled, but in 1920, women in Missouri and across the nation finally gained the right to vote when the 19th Amendment to the Constitution went into effect.

Some women also became more active in political life. In 1890, despite not being able to vote herself, Annie White Baxter of Carthage was elected clerk of Jasper County by male voters.

Other women became more involved in trying to change society. Many of them joined the Women's Christian **Temperance** Union, an organization that hoped to outlaw the sale of alcoholic beverages. One of these women, Carry Nation, hated alcohol so much that she would smash up bars with a hatchet. Most people, even within the temperance movement, did not support Nation's actions. The temperance movement was very successful for a time. In 1920, the period called Prohibition began when the 18th Amendment, which banned the sale and manufacture of alcohol, went into effect. It was repealed in 1933.

PROSPERITY AND DEPRESSION

In the years after World War I, Missouri prospered. Industry boomed, and Missourians were eager to enjoy many new inventions. They went to the movies, bought radios, and played records. People packed the jazz clubs of Kansas City.

A popular song of the day said that "anything goes." That was certainly true in Kansas City in the early 20th century. Gambling was common, and even during Prohibition, the city's saloons sold alcohol. This was due in large part to Thomas Pendergast and his influence on the city's officials.

But trouble was on the horizon. In 1929, the New York stock market collapsed. Banks couldn't lend money. People who had put their savings in banks lost their money. The Great Depression had begun.

Many factories in Missouri shut down, and people lost their jobs. Farmers in Missouri suffered, too. People had no money, so they couldn't afford to buy food. This meant that farmers couldn't sell their crops. Without money to pay the banks for their farms, many farmers lost their land. In the Ozarks, many people relied on hunting to feed their families.

To make matters worse, a severe drought struck the Great Plains, which stretches into western Missouri. The area became known as the Dust Bowl because the topsoil dried up and the wind blew it away. So much dust swirled in the air that it was sometimes dark at noon.

MINI-BIO

THOMAS PENDERGAST: THE BOSS OF KANSAS CITY

Born in St. Joseph, Missouri, Thomas Pendergast (1872–1945) moved to Kansas City in the 1890s to work for his brother, who taught him about the city's political system. Following his brother's lead, the younger Pendergast was soon controlling local elections by tampering with ballots and elections. In this way, he kept friends in office, who in return awarded Pendergast's companies with building contracts. The "Pendergast machine" essentially ran the local Democratic Party that got everything it wanted from about 1924 to 1939. In 1939, the federal government finally arrested and imprisoned him for income tax evasion.

? **Want to know more?** Visit www.factsfornow.scholastic.com and enter the keyword **Missouri**.

FLYING SOLO

In 1919, a wealthy Frenchman offered a prize to anyone making the first nonstop flight from New York to Paris. Many people tried to win the prize, and many failed. A young pilot named Charles Lindbergh persuaded a group of St. Louis businessmen to pay for a specially designed airplane. Although the prize did not require that there be only one pilot, Lindbergh chose to fly solo. On May 20, 1927, Lindbergh took off from New York in an airplane named the *Spirit of St. Louis.* He landed safely near Paris, France, 33 hours and 30 minutes later, having traveled 3,610 miles (5,810 km). The flight made Lindbergh a hero. It also demonstrated that safe, intercontinental travel was possible, and it increased public and commercial interest in air travel.

Charles Lindbergh and the *Spirit of St. Louis*

The federal government under President Franklin Roosevelt tried to help people suffering during the Great Depression. It started programs such as the Civilian Conservation Corps (CCC), which put people to work building roads in national forests. In addition, many rural areas got electricity for the first time. Prior to this, only about 6 percent of Missouri farms had electricity.

In the 1920s, workers began building the Bagnell Dam across the Osage River, which was intended to provide electricity in the St. Louis area. When the Depression struck, jobless people came from all over the country to work on the dam. After it was finished in 1931, it formed the 129-mile-long (208 km) Lake of the Ozarks, one of the largest lakes in Missouri.

WORLD WAR II

Though such programs provided some relief, the United States did not begin to pull out of the Depression until World War II began in Europe. In 1939, Germany invaded neighboring Poland. Other European countries were soon overrun by German troops as well. France and Britain—both friends, or allies, of the United States—were fighting the Germans. Many Americans wanted the United States to stay out of the conflict. But after Japan, an ally of Germany, bombed the U.S. naval base at Pearl Harbor, Hawai'i, on December 7, 1941, the United States was at war.

When the war began, crop prices rose rapidly, helping farmers. Jobs in manufacturing multiplied, and new chemical plants opened. As men joined the armed forces, more women entered the workforce. Many got jobs making bullets, aircraft, and other wartime supplies.

Men and women building airplanes at the Curtiss-Wright Corporation in St. Louis during World War II

NAACP members protesting school segregation in St. Louis

WORD TO KNOW

segregated *separated from others, according to race, class, ethnic group, religion, or other factors*

Fort Leonard Wood was established in the Ozarks in 1940 as a training camp for soldiers. Thousands of workers completed 1,600 buildings in just seven months. During World War II, more than 300,000 troops trained at Fort Leonard Wood.

In April 1945, President Roosevelt died. Vice President Harry S Truman, a Missourian, became president. In August 1945, he ordered that atomic bombs be dropped on the Japanese cities of Hiroshima and Nagasaki. The bombs leveled the cities and eventually killed more than 200,000 people. Six days after the second bomb was dropped, the Japanese surrendered. The war was over.

THE STRUGGLE FOR EQUALITY

During World War II, African Americans took on many jobs that had not been available to them before. They hoped that they would still be able to find jobs when the war ended and the white soldiers came home. After the war, African Americans from all over Missouri moved to St. Louis and Kansas City looking for work. Most ended up living in areas separate from whites.

In Missouri, white and black Americans were **segregated** in many areas. In 1896, the U.S. Supreme Court had ruled that it was legal to have separate facilities for African Americans so long as they were "equal" to facilities for white Americans. As a result, African Americans attended separate schools, rode in separate train cars, and played on separate playgrounds.

However, the facilities for African Americans were never actually equal to those for whites. In the 1930s, the National Association for the Advancement of Colored People (NAACP) began filing court cases challenging segregation laws. When the law school at the University of Missouri rejected Lloyd Gaines because he was black, the

NAACP took Gaines's case to court. In 1938, the Supreme Court ordered Missouri to admit Gaines to the university or provide another school of equal stature within the state.

Slowly, segregation in Missouri broke down. In 1947, the Catholic Church ended segregation in Catholic schools. Soon thereafter, St. Louis churches stopped segregating the congregations during church services. But some white Missourians resisted the changes. In 1949, riots broke out in St. Louis when people of color were admitted to the public swimming pools and playgrounds.

In 1954, the U.S. Supreme Court ruled that segregated schools were not lawful. Missouri's African Americans hoped that this would bring about swift change, but the courts did not demand that Missouri desegregate its public schools until 1980.

In 1948, President Harry Truman ordered that the U.S. military end segregation within its ranks.

MINI-BIO

LUCILE BLUFORD: JOURNALIST AND ACTIVIST

Lucile Harris Bluford (1911–2003) grew up in Kansas City. She wanted to become a journalist, but Missouri's journalism school refused to admit her because she was African American. So instead, she enrolled at the University of Kansas. After graduating, she became an editor and publisher of the *Kansas City Call*, a black-owned newspaper. In 1939, Bluford applied to do graduate work at the University of Missouri School of Journalism. She was turned down—11 times. In 1941, the state supreme court ruled that the university must admit her. Instead, the university shut down its graduate journalism program. Almost 50 years later, the school that had rejected her awarded her an honorary doctorate.

? **Want to know more?** Visit www.factsfornow .scholastic.com and enter the keyword **Missouri**.

Over time, African Americans in Missouri gained political power. In 1968, William Clay was elected to the U.S. Congress from a district in St. Louis. He was the state's first black congressman.

RISING TOURISM

The Ozarks were poor, rugged backcountry through most of history. The people who lived in these mountains had few ways of making a living, and they rarely visited larger towns. Then, in the 1950s, the White River was dammed in several places to prevent flooding. The last of the dams, Table Rock Dam, was completed in 1958, forming Table Rock Lake. Tourists were soon coming to the lake to enjoy the beautiful scenery.

Branson, located near Table Rock Lake, became the heart of the Ozarks' tourist industry. The town's first live show opened in 1958. Over the years, more and more theaters opened. By the 1980s, it was a center of country music, and since the early 2000s, it has been attracting some 8 million visitors a year.

CHANGING CITIES

Since 1900, nearly all the counties north of the Missouri River have decreased in population. One reason for the population decline is the increase in larger and more mechanized farms in the region. Fewer people are

Busy highways in St. Louis

needed to work the farms, so workers and their families are moving to cities and suburbs in larger numbers.
Cities offer better job opportunities, especially in high-
tech industries. They also offer higher quality healthcare
facilities and more varied entertainment. One exception
to this growth in cities is St. Louis, where the population
dropped from 856,796 in 1950 to 319,294 in 2010. During
that time, many St. Louis residents moved from the city to
the surrounding suburbs. Improved transportation helps
sustain this larger suburban population. Today, modern
highways stretch out for miles from major cities to suburban areas.

READ ABOUT

Fans gather to cheer
on the St. Louis
Cardinals in the
2013 World Series.

CHAPTER SIX

PEOPLE

★

MANY STATES HAVE NICKNAMES THAT REFER TO THEIR BEAUTY OR TO A NATURAL RESOURCE. But not Missouri. It is called the Show-Me State. This means that Missourians aren't swayed by long words. They need to see proof. Where did this nickname come from? No one knows for certain, but one story is that Congressman Willard Duncan Vandiver delivered a speech in 1899 during which he said, "I come from a state that raises corn and cotton and cockleburs and Democrats, and frothy eloquence neither convinces nor satisfies me. I am from Missouri. You have got to show me."

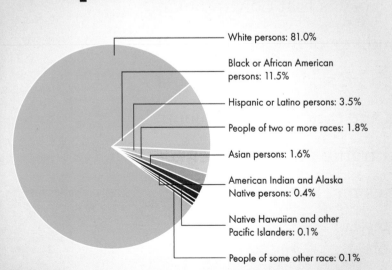

People QuickFacts

White persons: 81.0%

Black or African American persons: 11.5%

Hispanic or Latino persons: 3.5%

People of two or more races: 1.8%

Asian persons: 1.6%

American Indian and Alaska Native persons: 0.4%

Native Hawaiian and other Pacific Islanders: 0.1%

People of some other race: 0.1%

Source: U.S. Census Bureau, 2010 census

Missourians enjoying a day at Fair Saint Louis

WHO IS A MISSOURIAN?

Missourians are northerners, southerners, easterners, and westerners. They are farmers and city dwellers. About 70 percent of Missourians live in or near cities. The two biggest cities in Missouri are Kansas City, on the western side of the state, and St. Louis, on the eastern side.

More than four-fifths of Missourians are of European descent. The largest group traces its ancestry to Germany. The next-largest group is of Irish ancestry. Recent immigrants are more likely to be from eastern Europe. An estimated 70,000 Bosnians live in the St. Louis area. Many of them fled a war in their homeland in southeastern Europe in the 1990s.

People of Spanish descent have lived in Missouri since before it became a state. Today, about 3.5 percent of Missourians are Hispanic. Their numbers increased by

St. Patrick's Day performers in St. Louis

Participants prepare for the Hispanic Days ceremonies before a St. Louis Cardinals baseball game.

Where Missourians Live

The colors on this map indicate population density throughout the state.
The darker the color, the more people live there.

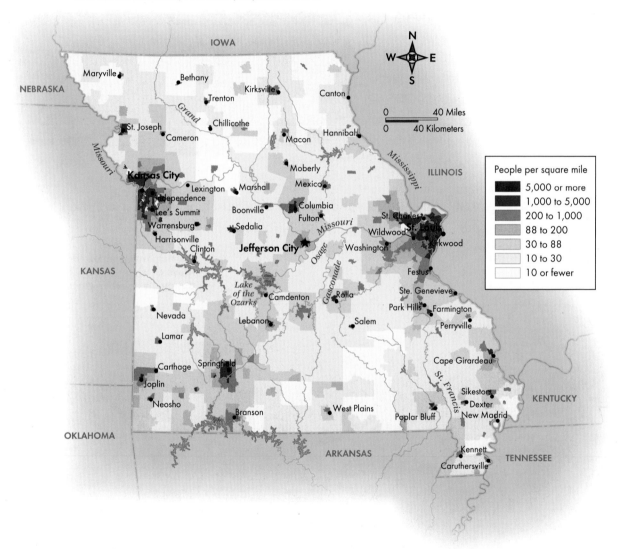

79 percent between 2000 and 2010. Much of the growth was in Kansas City. Most Hispanic Missourians are of Mexican descent. Others moved to Missouri from Puerto Rico, Cuba, and Central American nations such as El Salvador and Guatemala.

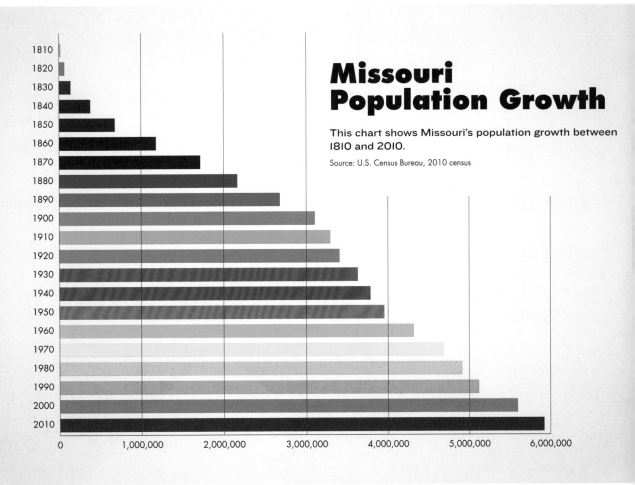

Missouri Population Growth

This chart shows Missouri's population growth between 1810 and 2010.

Source: U.S. Census Bureau, 2010 census

About half of St. Louis's population and 30 percent of Kansas City's population is African American. Many African Americans moved to these cities from all over the country for job opportunities.

People of Asian descent make up about 1.6 percent of Missouri's population. Most are of Vietnamese or Chinese descent. Others come from Middle Eastern countries such as Afghanistan, Iran, and Iraq.

Missouri is not home to any official American Indian reservations. Native Americans were forced to move from Missouri into Oklahoma and Kansas more than 150 years

Big City Life

This list shows the population of Missouri's biggest cities.

Kansas City 459,787
St. Louis 319,294
Springfield 159,498
Independence 116,830
Columbia 108,500

Source: U.S. Census Bureau, 2010 census

ago. A few Native Americans stayed, however. The Lost Cherokees settled in southeastern Missouri in the early 1700s. Today, they call themselves the Northern Cherokee Nation of the Old Louisiana Territory, and they are sprinkled throughout Missouri and Arkansas. Their headquarters is in Columbia.

EDUCATION

Missouri has long valued education. The French community of Ste. Genevieve established a school for poor children, both white and Native American, as early as 1806. In

A group of students studying in the main library at Washington University

1839, the state created a public education system, though the state's first high school wasn't established until 1853, in St. Louis. After the Civil War, Missouri laws required that all children—both white and non-white—go to public school.

Missourians approved the idea of charter schools in 1998. These are public schools that do not have to follow the rules that regular public schools do. Today, there are more than 30 charter schools in Missouri. So far, they are allowed only in St. Louis and Kansas City. In St. Louis, the mayor hopes that good charter schools will draw people back to living in the city.

The Jesuits, a Catholic order, founded St. Louis University in 1818, making it the first university west of the Mississippi. Twenty-one years later, the University of Missouri became the first state university west of the Mississippi.

Washington University in St. Louis is a private university. Its medical school is one of the finest in the country. At least 23 winners of the Nobel Prize in Medicine have taught there.

Black soldiers coming home from the Civil War established a college for African Americans, which became Lincoln University in Jefferson City. Today, the school educates students of all races.

MINI-BIO

SUSAN BLOW: INNOVATIVE EDUCATOR

Susan Elizabeth Blow (1843–1916) grew up in a wealthy St. Louis family. After the Civil War, she had the good fortune to travel to Germany. There she visited classrooms inspired by the ideas of educator Friedrich Froebel. He had shown that young children learn important skills by playing with balls, blocks, and other toys. He thought that schools should provide this sort of education to the very young. He called his idea a kindergarten, which is German for "garden of children." Susan Blow took Froebel's idea back to St. Louis and opened the first public kindergarten in the United States in 1873. Within 10 years, every public school in St. Louis had a kindergarten.

? **Want to know more?** Visit www.factsfornow .scholastic.com and enter the keyword **Missouri**.

HOW TO TALK LIKE A MISSOURIAN

Most sports fans know that Mizzou (pronounced mih-ZOO) is the University of Missouri–Columbia. But Missourians also have other unique words and phrases. Here are a few:

The Lou — slang for St. Louis

Mound City — a nickname for St. Louis, coming from the Native American burial mounds once built in the city

HOW TO EAT LIKE A MISSOURIAN

Missouri sits at the crossroads of America, and this is reflected in the foods Missourians eat. They enjoy southern treats such as pecan pie. They also eat foods typical of the West. Beef and barbecue are popular in Kansas City, which was once the site of a major stockyard. Missouri's rivers also play a large role in how Missourians eat. Catfish is a popular catch in the state's rivers and lakes. Missourians also enjoy fresh produce from local farms.

A farmers' market in St. Louis

Artist Rose O'Neill's family moved from Pennsylvania to the Ozarks, near Branson. She designed a cute figure that she thought looked like Cupid, so she called it the Kewpie doll. First appearing in 1910, Kewpie dolls quickly became popular in the United States and Europe.

In recent decades, the Ozarks have become a popular tourist destination. This has helped revive the craft of wood carving, which had almost died out. Peter Engler played a large role in that revival. In 1962, he opened a wood-carving shop in Branson, where he specialized in making traditional Santa Claus figures. Many other wood-carvers have also set up shop in Branson.

MUSICIANS

Missouri has long been a center of musical innovation. Ragtime, perhaps the first type of music invented in the United States, was popular in the late 19th and early 20th centuries. Ragtime stresses musical notes between the regular beats, called syncopation, which is common in traditional African music. Scott Joplin, a pianist and composer from Sedalia, was the "King of Ragtime."

Around the same time, jazz was also developing. Kansas City was an early center for jazz. Like ragtime, jazz uses syncopation, but it also uses improvisation. Performers make up some of the music as they go along. First one musician solos, and then another, almost as if they are having a conversation.

MINI-BIO

SCOTT JOPLIN: KING OF RAGTIME

Scott Joplin (c. 1867–1917) was born in Texas and began playing piano as a young child. He eventually settled in Sedalia, where he studied music at George R. Smith College. In the 1890s, he developed the style that became ragtime. In 1899, he wrote "Maple Leaf Rag"—named for an African American social club in Sedalia—and it was a huge success. This encouraged him to move to St. Louis, where he wrote masterpieces such as "The Entertainer," which was used as the theme song for the movie The Sting, and "Ragtime Dance." In 1976, long after his death, Joplin was awarded a Pulitzer Prize for his contributions to American music.

? **Want to know more?** Visit www.factsfornow .scholastic.com and enter the keyword **Missouri**.

Charlie "Bird" Parker, Coleman Hawkins, Fletcher Henderson, Count Basie, and Mary Lou Williams were Kansas City jazz favorites starting in the 1930s. Their style, which is relaxed and uses complicated improvisations, became known as Kansas City jazz. St. Louis singer Josephine Baker performed many kinds of music, including jazz. After moving to Paris, France, in 1925, she became one of the biggest stars in Europe.

St. Louis is an important center of blues music. Today, it is the home of the National Blues Museum.

MINI-BIO

JOSEPHINE BAKER: ENTERTAINER AND ACTIVIST

Josephine Baker (1906–1975) began her career dancing in the streets of her hometown of St. Louis when she was a child. By the time she was a teenager, she was performing in Broadway musicals in New York. Her popularity took her to Paris, France, where she became a top dancer in Paris nightclubs. In 1927, she earned more money than any other entertainer in Europe. Returning often to the United States, she actively supported the struggle for equality and refused to appear before segregated audiences. When she died in Paris in 1975, 20,000 people turned out for her funeral procession.

? Want to know more? Visit www.factsfornow .scholastic.com and enter the keyword **Missouri**.

Rapper Nelly is from St. Louis.

Musician Sheryl Crow grew up in Kennett.

MARK TWAIN: NOVELIST

Mark Twain (1835–1910), one of the country's greatest novelists, was born Samuel Clemens in Florida, Missouri. He grew up in Hannibal, which was a slave-trading center. Twain's father owned slaves, and young Sam never forgot seeing his father sell a slave away "from his home, his mother, and his friends." Twain once wrote that slavery was "maintained by the lie of silent asser-tion—the silent assertion that there wasn't anything going on in which humane and intelligent people were interested." Twain placed Jim, an enslaved man desperately running to freedom, at the center of his classic novel *The Adventures of Huckleberry Finn*. Throughout his life, Twain denounced oppression of all kinds.

 Want to know more? Visit www.factsfornow.scholastic.com and enter the keyword **Missouri**.

More recently, Missouri has produced musicians who work in many different styles. Nelly, who grew up as Cornell Haynes Jr. in St. Louis, is one of the best-selling rappers of all time. Sheryl Crow, an award-winning singer and songwriter, grew up in Kennett, in southeastern Missouri.

WRITERS

No writer is more closely associated with Missouri than the humorist-novelist Mark Twain. He used his Missouri childhood in his classic novels *The Adventures of Tom Sawyer* and *The Adventures of Huckleberry Finn*.

WORD TO KNOW

feminist *holding the belief that women are the political, economic, and social equals of men*

St. Louis-born Kate Chopin wrote *The Awakening,* an early **feminist** novel about a woman who is trapped by her role as wife and mother. Born in Columbus, Mississippi, playwright Tennessee Williams and his family moved to St. Louis when he was seven. He set his play *The Glass Menagerie,* about a young man trying to deal with his controlling mother and his desperately shy sister, in that city. Williams eventually won two Pulitzer Prizes, first for *The Glass Menagerie* and then for *Cat on a Hot Tin Roof.* Maya Angelou recounted her rough St. Louis childhood in books such as *I Know Why the Caged Bird Sings.* Children's writer Laura Ingalls Wilder also drew on her own childhood when writing her beloved Little House series.

Joseph Pulitzer founded the *St. Louis Post-Dispatch,* the biggest newspaper in Missouri. In his will, Pulitzer estab-

Playwright Tennessee Williams writing at his desk in 1948

Journalist and publisher Joseph Pulitzer

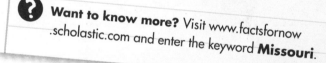

MINI-BIO

MAYA ANGELOU: POET AND NOVELIST

Maya Angelou (1928–2014) was named Marguerite Johnson when she was born in St. Louis. After her parents divorced, she moved frequently, living sometimes with her grandmother in Arkansas and sometimes with her mother in Missouri or California. Beginning at age eight, Angelou refused to speak for five years because she thought her words had caused a man to be murdered. She later became a singer, actor, dancer, newspaper editor, poet, and civil rights worker. Her complicated life provided the material for six autobiographical novels, including *I Know Why the Caged Bird Sings* and *All God's Children Need Traveling Shoes*.

❓ Want to know more? Visit www.factsfornow.scholastic.com and enter the keyword **Missouri**.

lished prizes for outstanding journalism and literary writing. The first Pulitzer Prizes were awarded in 1917. Prizes were later added in other fields such as music.

Missouri has also produced many innovative poets. T. S. Eliot, who grew up in a prominent St. Louis family, was a giant of modern poetry. His long poem *The Waste Land,* published in 1922, expressed the frustration and restlessness felt by many young people at the time. Eliot received the Nobel Prize in Literature, the world's highest literary honor, in 1948. Mona Van Duyn, a longtime teacher at Washington University in St. Louis, became the first female U.S. poet laureate in 1992. Another Missouri poet, Marianne Moore, used precise language to describe images from nature.

MISSOURI SPORTS

Missourians are crazy about sports. Football fans cheer on the St. Louis Rams and the Kansas City Chiefs, hockey fans thrill to the slapshots of the St. Louis Blues, while soccer fans root for the Kansas City Wizards.

The St. Louis Cardinals are the state's oldest professional sports team. They have been around since 1882, when they were called the St. Louis Brown Stockings. Unlike most Major League Baseball teams, the Cardinals

Members of the Kansas City Wizards soccer team celebrate a goal against the Colorado Rapids.

Fans taking in a St. Louis Cardinals game

have remained in the same city throughout their history. As of 2011, the Cards had won the World Series 11 times, more than any other team except the New York Yankees.

In Kansas City, baseball fans root for the Royals. In 1985, Missourians were thrilled when the Royals faced the Cardinals in the World Series. The two top teams in baseball were both from the Show-Me State.

MINI-BIO

CHARLES "CASEY" STENGEL: THE OLD PROFESSOR

Charles "Casey" Stengel (1890–1975), born in Kansas City, was one of the most beloved and colorful figures in baseball history. From 1912 to 1925, he played for the Brooklyn Dodgers, Pittsburgh Pirates, Philadelphia Phillies, New York Giants, and Boston Braves. After retiring, Stengel—nicknamed "The Old Professor" because of his vast baseball knowledge—turned to managing. In 12 years as manager of the New York Yankees, he led the team to an incredible five World Series victories in a row (1949–1953). Stengel was inducted into the Baseball Hall of Fame in 1966.

❓ Want to know more? Visit www.factsfornow.scholastic.com and enter the keyword **Missouri**.

READ ABOUT

The Missouri House
of Representatives
in session in 2014

CHAPTER SEVEN

GOVERNMENT

★

T HE MISSOURI STATE GOVERNMENT, CONVINCED THAT EVERY CHILD IS "BORN TO LEARN," BEGAN A PROGRAM CALLED PARENTS AS TEACHERS IN 1981. It helps organizations identify children who might need extra help before they get to kindergarten and then teaches parents how to help their children learn. Families can take part when their children are as young as six months old. Parents as Teachers is now a successful national organization, but it all began with the work of the Missouri government and the local schools.

Capitol Facts

Here are some fascinating facts about Missouri's state capitol.

Number of stories: 5

Length: 437 feet (133 m)

Width at center: 300 feet (91 m)

Width of wings: 200 feet (61 m)

Height: 262 feet (80 m) from basement floor

Diameter of dome: 90 feet (27 m)

Cost in 1911: $4 million

Statue on top: Ceres, goddess of agriculture in ancient Roman mythology

The capitol in Jefferson City

THE CENTER OF GOVERNMENT

The capital of Missouri is Jefferson City. It is named after President Thomas Jefferson, who made the Louisiana Purchase. Missouri's first General Assembly chose the capital's location, which is in the center of the state. Lawmakers hoped that putting the capital there would prevent the state's growing population from concentrating in the north.

The first capitol was built in 1826. It was only 40 by 60 feet (12 by 18 m), about the size of an average house today, but it served as both the governor's home and the place where the legislature met. The capitol was destroyed by fire in 1837. A second, much larger capitol was soon built. In 1911, it, too, was destroyed by fire, as were many of the state's records and documents.

A new, grand capitol was not completed until 1924. This capitol, which still stands today, is covered in marble mined at Carthage, near Kansas City. In 1935, Thomas Hart Benton painted four huge murals in the capitol.

Capital City

This map shows places of interest in Jefferson City, Missouri's capital city.

Together, they are called *Social History of the State of Missouri*. The murals depict both average people and characters from American folktales.

The current Missouri constitution was adopted in 1945. It divides the state government into three branches: executive, legislative, and judicial.

EXECUTIVE BRANCH

The executive branch is in charge of carrying out the laws of the state. The governor heads it and appoints the leaders of state agencies. He or she also signs bills into law or vetoes bills, preventing them from becoming law. The governor must be at least 30 years old and have lived in Missouri for 10 years. A governor can serve only two four-year terms.

Missouri State Government

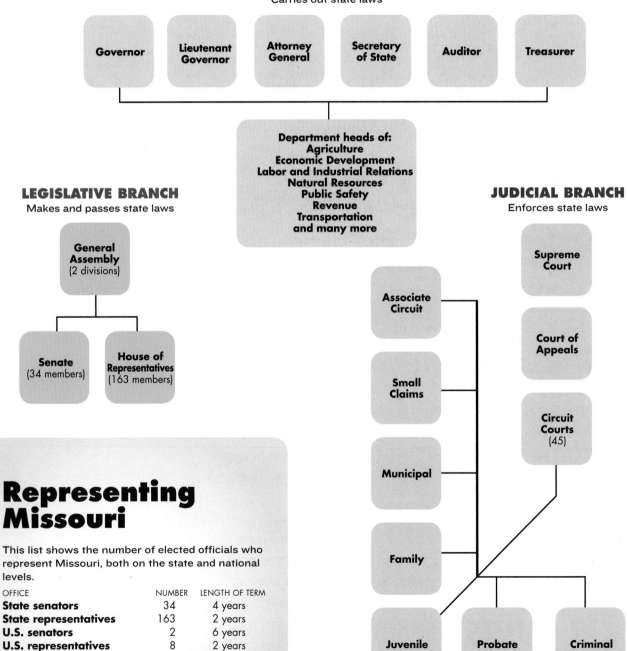

EXECUTIVE BRANCH
Carries out state laws

Governor

Lieutenant Governor

Attorney General

Secretary of State

Auditor

Treasurer

Department heads of:
Agriculture
Economic Development
Labor and Industrial Relations
Natural Resources
Public Safety
Revenue
Transportation
and many more

LEGISLATIVE BRANCH
Makes and passes state laws

General Assembly (2 divisions)

Senate (34 members)

House of Representatives (163 members)

JUDICIAL BRANCH
Enforces state laws

Supreme Court

Court of Appeals

Circuit Courts (45)

Associate Circuit

Small Claims

Municipal

Family

Juvenile

Probate

Criminal

Representing Missouri

This list shows the number of elected officials who represent Missouri, both on the state and national levels.

OFFICE	NUMBER	LENGTH OF TERM
State senators	34	4 years
State representatives	163	2 years
U.S. senators	2	6 years
U.S. representatives	8	2 years
Presidential electors	10	—

The lieutenant governor is also elected to a four-year term, but there are no limits on how many terms he or she can serve. The lieutenant governor is also president of the state senate. He or she also takes over as governor if the governor dies or leaves office.

The attorney general is the chief lawyer for the state. He or she helps the police fight crime and represents the state in legal matters. Other top positions in the executive branch are state auditor, who oversees how the state's money is being spent, and state treasurer, who is in charge of collecting taxes and investing the state's money.

LEGISLATIVE BRANCH

The legislative branch makes the laws of the state. As a whole, it is called the Missouri General Assembly, but it is divided into two bodies—the house of representatives and the senate. The house of representatives has 163 members who serve two-year terms. The senate has 34 members who serve four-year terms. In 1992, Missouri's constitution was changed so that no representative or senator can serve more than eight years. The legislature meets only from January to May each year, which gives the representatives and senators time to hold other jobs.

HARRY S TRUMAN: MISSOURI'S PRESIDENT

Harry S Truman (1884–1972) was born in Lamar and raised in Independence, a city that became his lifelong home. He served as a captain in World War I. After he came home, he soon became involved in politics. He served as a U.S. senator and then vice president under President Franklin D. Roosevelt. But on April 12, 1945, Roosevelt died. Truman was now president. He led the nation through the end of World War II and was elected to a second term in 1948. Truman's time as president was difficult. He had to deal with angry workers at home and wars abroad. But he would never blame others for his problems or decisions. Referring to the saying "passing the buck," he said, that, as president, "The buck stops here."

 Want to know more? Visit www.factsfornow .scholastic.com and enter the keyword **Missouri**.

JUDICIAL BRANCH

The judicial branch consists of the state's court system. The court system has three levels: circuit courts, the court of appeals, and the supreme court. Most trials are held in Missouri's 45 circuit courts. Someone who believes a circuit court made a mistake can ask the Missouri Court of Appeals to review the case. The state has three appeals courts, in St. Louis, Kansas City, and Springfield. The Missouri Supreme Court reviews decisions of the appeals courts. It also hears any cases involving the state constitution, the death penalty, or U.S. treaties. The governor appoints the supreme court's seven judges, but each judge must be approved by a vote of the people after one year in office. The judges serve 12-year terms.

LOCAL GOVERNMENT

Missouri is divided into 114 counties and the city of St. Louis. There is also a county of St. Louis, but the city is not part of it. St. Louis County is the state's largest county by population. The smallest county by both size and population is Worth County in the northwest. It has difficulty drawing in enough tax money to pay for

THINK ABOUT IT!

Combining City and Suburb

The city of St. Louis is governed separately from St. Louis County. This is a highly uncommon situation. Some people in the St. Louis area have considered the idea of merging the city of St. Louis with St. Louis County to become one big city. If that happened, St. Louis would be one of the nation's 10 largest cities.

Why do it? Because the social and economic problems St. Louis faces don't stop at the city limits. Issues related to jobs, transportation, education, and crime affect both city and suburb, so the local governments may be more effective at solving problems if they work on them as one entity. One area where the merger may help is education. In 2007, the city's public schools were taken over by the state because they were performing so poorly. Many people believe a merger would provide city schools with additional funds and resources.

Some people in the suburbs are opposed to the merger because they are afraid it would raise their taxes. One writer, talking to people in the suburbs, argued, "There are a million reasons why [the separation of city and suburb] is bad for the residents of St. Louis, but it is also bad for you. If you were part of St. Louis, it would only take a very, very small portion of your money to solve what is a very bad problem. And it's not like it's someone else's problem. It's your problem, because it's just right across the freeway and social problems don't respect city lines."

Missouri Counties

This map shows the 114 counties in Missouri, plus the independent city of St. Louis. Jefferson City, the state capital, is indicated with a star.

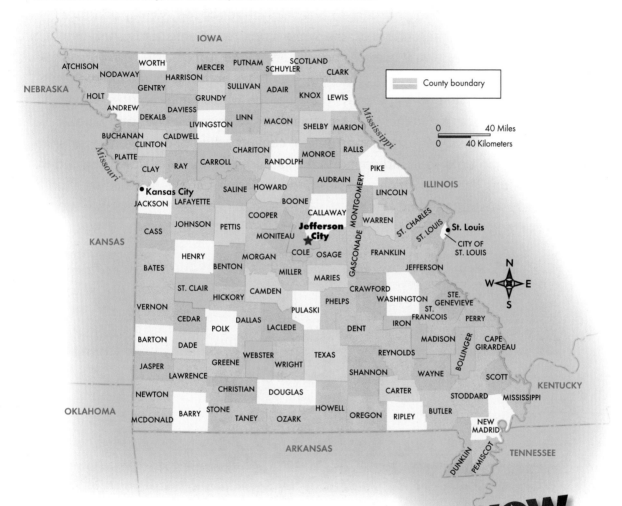

county services. In 2007, some people were suggesting that Worth County should merge with another nearby county. On the other side of the state, some people are suggesting that the city of St. Louis merge with St. Louis County. They argue that the combined government would be better able to serve its citizens.

WOW

In 2000, Jean Carnahan became the first woman to represent Missouri in the U.S. Senate. She was appointed in place of her husband, Governor Mel Carnahan, who was elected despite having died three weeks before the election.

State Flag

The Missouri state flag has three horizontal stripes of red, white, and blue. The red stripe represents valor; the white stripe represents purity; and the blue stripe represents vigilance, permanency, and justice. The Missouri state seal appears in the center of the flag, signifying both Missouri's independence as a state and its place as a part of the whole United States. Having the state seal in the center of the national colors of red, white, and blue shows that Missouri is the geographical center of the nation. Twenty-four stars encircle the state seal, indicating that Missouri was the 24th state admitted to the Union. The flag, which was designed by Cape Girardeau resident Marie Oliver, was adopted in 1913.

State Seal

In the middle of the Missouri state seal is a shield. On the right side of the shield, a bald eagle grasps the olive branches of peace and the arrows of war in its talons. This represents the strength and powers of the federal government. On the left side of the shield are a grizzly bear and a crescent moon. The bear symbolizes the strength and bravery of Missourians. The moon symbolizes the possibility of a greater future. A belt inscribed with "United we stand, divided we fall" encircles the shield.

Two more grizzly bears are on opposite sides of the shield. They stand on a scroll inscribed with the state motto, *Salus populi suprema lex esto*, which is Latin for "Let the welfare of the people be the supreme law." Above the shield is a helmet, which symbolizes that Missouri is a strong, independent state. Above this is a large star surrounded by 24 smaller stars, signifying that Missouri was the 24th state.

Robert Wells—a lawyer, state legislator, and judge—designed the seal. It was adopted on January 11, 1822.

READ ABOUT

CHUTE FILLER STORAGE

Workers at the Baldor
Electric Company
factory in St. Louis

CHAPTER EIGHT

ECONOMY

★

M ISSOURI SITS AT THE CROSS-
ROADS OF THE NATION. Trucks,
trains, airplanes, and barges head
out from Missouri to points across the country.
Kansas City is the nation's third-largest truck
terminal. St. Louis is the nation's second-largest
inland port. These trucks and trains carry
factory goods and farm products from one part
of the country to another, but manufacturing
and agriculture no longer dominate the Missouri
economy. Instead, services play the largest role.

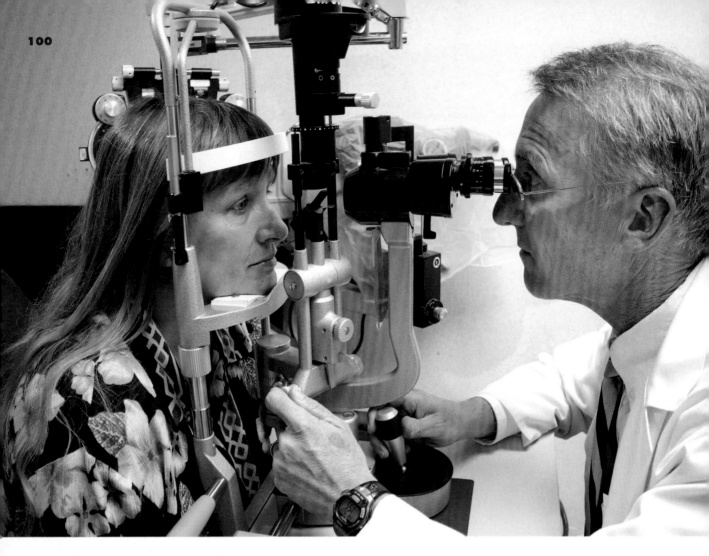

An ophthalmologist checks a patient's eyes at the Mason Eye Institute at the University of Missouri.

C. H. Laessig built the world's first gasoline station in St. Louis in 1905. His customers were able to fill their tanks through a garden hose rather than buying gasoline by the can.

SERVICE INDUSTRIES

The vast majority of Missourians work in service industries. They don't make or grow a product. Instead, they do work that helps others. Bank tellers, teachers, gas station attendants, bus drivers, and lawyers all work in service industries.

In Missouri, health care, education, and tourism are among the largest service industries. Millions of people visit Branson every year to enjoy live music in a beautiful setting. The finance and real estate industries are also important. H&R Block, the nation's leading tax preparation company, is headquartered in Kansas City.

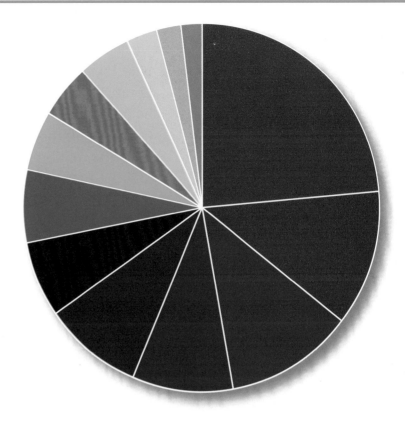

What Do Missourians Do?

This color-coded chart shows what industries Missourians work in.

23.8%	Educational services, and health care and social assistance 661,221
11.9%	Retail trade 331,693
11.7%	Manufacturing 324,797
9.0%	Professional, scientific, and management, and administrative and waste management services 250,569

8.9%	Arts, entertainment, and recreation, and accommodation and food services 248,811
6.9%	Finance and insurance, and real estate and rental and leasing 191,851
6.4%	Construction 178,324
5.1%	Transportation and warehousing, and utilities 142,390

4.8%	Other services, except public administration 134,871
4.7%	Public administration 129,487
2.8%	Wholesale trade 78,877
2.2%	Information 60,106
1.8%	Agriculture, forestry, fishing and hunting, and mining 48,794

Source: U.S. Census Bureau, 2010 census

MANUFACTURING

Manufacturing accounts for about 12 percent of Missouri's employment. The state's major manufacturing products include chemicals and transportation equipment such as motor vehicles, railroad cars, and airplanes. Many Missouri products are exported to other countries. By far the largest category of exports is transportation equipment, such as engines and vehicle assembly. Most of the exports go to Canada.

St. Louis's 10-story-tall Wainwright Building is considered one of the world's first skyscrapers. Built in 1891, the building was named for Missouri businessman Ellis Wainwright.

The nation's largest brewery, or beer-making business, is Anheuser-Busch, which is headquartered in St. Louis. Eberhard Anheuser, an immigrant from Germany, bought a small brewery in 1860. Four years later, his son-in-law, Adolphus Busch, joined him in the business. They were the first brewers to **pasteurize** beer to keep it fresh and the first to use refrigerated railway cars to transport their beer. Though Anheuser-Busch was purchased in 2008 by international beverage company InBev, it remains headquartered in St. Louis.

Monsanto Company doesn't produce food, but its work affects the food you eat. John Francis Queeny founded the company in 1901 in St. Louis. His first product was saccharin, an artificial sweetener. In recent years, the company has been altering the **genes** in seeds to improve crops. Monsanto is one of the nation's top 10 chemical companies.

WORDS TO KNOW

pasteurize *to heat a liquid in order to kill germs in it*

genes *chemicals in plants and animals that determine the traits passed from one generation to the next*

JOYCE C. HALL: THE MAN WHO "CARED ENOUGH"

Joyce C. Hall (1891–1982) was a Nebraskan who moved to Kansas City as a teenager. Determined to start a business for himself, he arrived with shoe boxes full of postcards, which he sold door-to-door. After his brother joined him, they started a company that made greeting cards. In 1954, the Hall Brothers Company became Hallmark. Hall believed firmly in advertising. In the mid-20th century, it seemed that all Americans knew the company slogan, "When you care enough to send the very best." Hallmark, the world's largest greeting card company, is still headquartered in Kansas City.

❓ **Want to know more?** Visit www.factsfornow .scholastic.com and enter the keyword **Missouri**.

In 1929, Charles L. Grigg of St. Louis invented the soft drink he called Bib-Label Lithiated Lemon-Lime Soda. He changed its name to the more catchy 7UP two years later.

Major Agricultural and Mining Products

This map shows where Missouri's major agricultural and mining products come from. See a chicken? That's where poultry is raised.

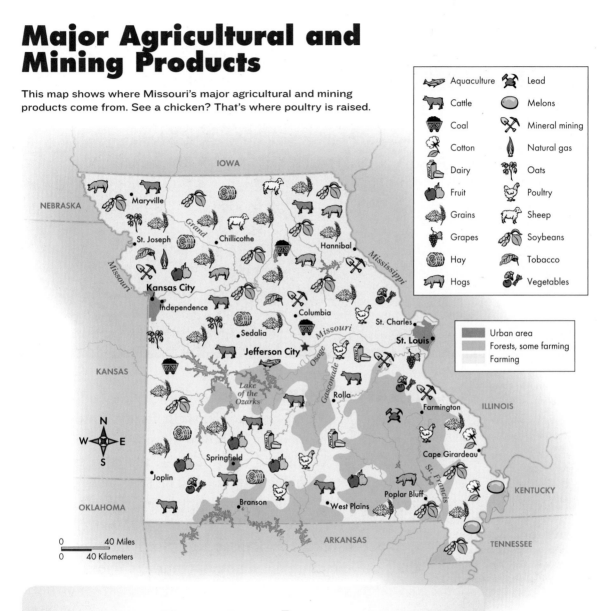

Aquaculture · Lead
Cattle · Melons
Coal · Mineral mining
Cotton · Natural gas
Dairy · Oats
Fruit · Poultry
Grains · Sheep
Grapes · Soybeans
Hay · Tobacco
Hogs · Vegetables

Urban area
Forests, some farming
Farming

Top Products

Manufacturing	Transportation equipment, processed foods, chemicals
Mining	Lead, limestone and crushed stone, coal, copper, silver, zinc
Agriculture	Soybeans, corn, cotton, wheat, apples, peaches
Livestock	Cattle, hogs, dairy products, turkeys

Dairy cows grazing in a Missouri field

A pecan farm in Brunswick in north-central Missouri boasts the World's Largest Pecan. The giant concrete nut weighs about 12,000 pounds (5,400 kg).

WORD TO KNOW

equine *related to the horse family*

AGRICULTURE

Missouri is second only to Texas in its total number of farms—it has more than 100,000 of them. The state's major crops are soybeans and corn. Most of the corn grown in Missouri is used to feed livestock. The state also produces hay, cotton, wheat, sorghum, apples, and pecans.

Livestock accounts for much of Missouri's farm income. Though the Kansas City Stockyards closed in 1991, cattle remain the state's number-one livestock product. Most of the state's cattle are raised on the northern plains and the Osage Prairie. Missouri also produces large numbers of hogs, chickens, and turkeys.

Missouri ranks among the top states in the nation in sales of **equine** animals. Hundreds of Missouri breeders sell all types of horses. One popular breed, the Missouri fox trotter, comes from the Ozarks. Pioneers found this strong horse useful on the rocky ground of the Ozarks.

When William Becknell established the Santa Fe Trail in 1821, he brought back some hardy Mexican mules and donkeys. Missouri farmers bred them into the famed Missouri mule. The Missouri mule is a cross between a female draft horse and a male donkey. Missouri was known around the world for the quality and quantity of its mules. Several Missouri companies still breed and sell mules. Trail riders in rough country sometimes prefer mules because they are more sure-footed than horses

MINING

Missouri has long been the nation's top lead-producing state. Most of the state's lead mines are in or near the St. Francois Mountains. Zinc, iron, and copper are found in Missouri. The state's other important mining products include crushed stone, lime, and sand and gravel.

SEE IT HERE!

AN UNDERGROUND WORLD
The Hunt Midwest SubTropolis in north Kansas City is the world's largest underground storage facility. This 1,100-acre (445 hectare) site is located in a cave created by limestone mining. Additional acres are added to the site every year as the mining continues. Companies rent space in the SubTropolis for use as offices and warehouses. Nearly 7 miles (11 km) of paved and lighted roads and 2 miles (3 km) of railroad tracks run through the facility, which has parking for 1,800 employees. The U.S. Postal Service is the facility's largest tenant.

Missouri mules transporting materials near the Panama Canal in 1940

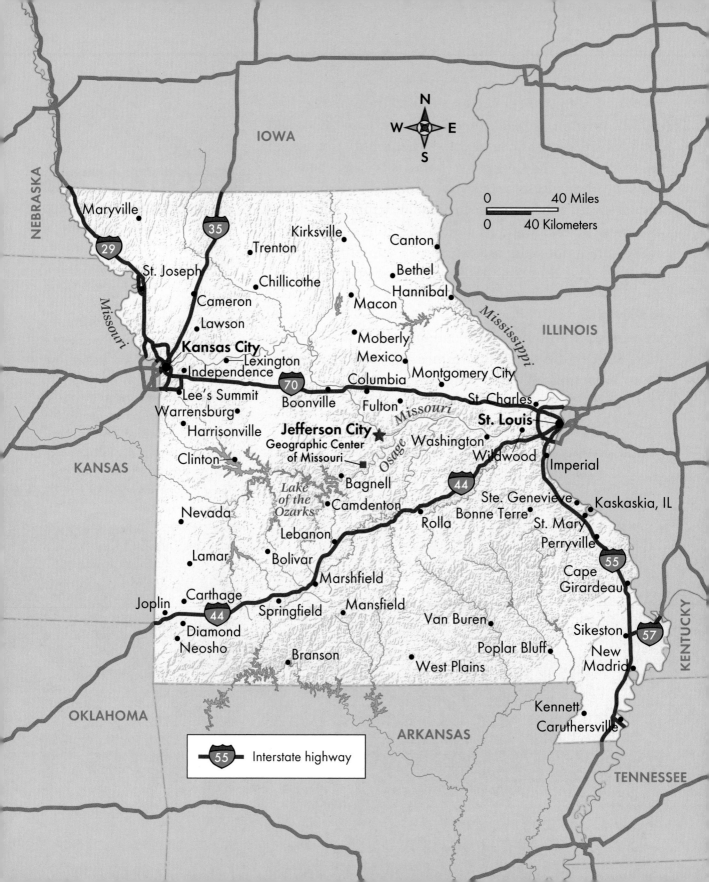

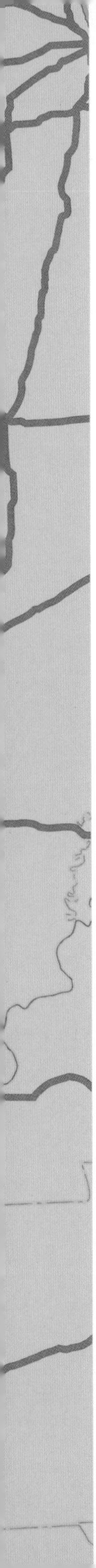

TRAVEL GUIDE

TRAVEL GUIDE

★

FROM THE LUSH FORESTS OF THE OZARKS TO THE COBBLESTONE STREETS OF OLD ST. LOUIS, THE STATE OF MISSOURI IS A GREAT PLACE TO EXPLORE. It's time to put on your walking shoes and visit some Indian mounds, see where Mark Twain grew up, and hear some jazz. There's no time to waste—grab your map and let's go!

←—Follow along with this travel map. We'll begin in Canton and travel all the way around the state to Independence!

ALONG THE MISSISSIPPI

THINGS TO DO: Ride a ferry across the Mississippi, have your picture taken next to Huck Finn, and see where ancient Indians lived.

Canton

★ **Canton Ferry:** The ferry at Canton is the longest continuously operating ferry service on the Mississippi. It has been carrying people and vehicles across the river to Meyer, Illinois, since 1853.

Hannibal

★ **Mark Twain Boyhood Home & Museum:** Discover what life was like for Mark Twain growing up in the small town of Hannibal. You can tour Twain's house and several other historic buildings. And don't miss the statue of Tom Sawyer and Huck Finn. Missouri sculptor Frederick C. Hibbard created it in 1926.

Montgomery City

★ **Graham Cave State Park:** Here you can explore where Native Americans lived 10,000 years ago.

Bethel

★ **Historic Bethel German Colony:** At this site, you can see how an immigrant community lived in the 1840s. More than 30 of the colony's original buildings are still standing, including a school and a tailor shop.

ST. LOUIS AREA

THINGS TO DO: Catch a Cardinals game, take a trip to the top of the country's highest monument, and say hello to a hippo.

★ **The Gateway Arch:** This symbol of St. Louis soars 630 feet (192 m) high, taller than any other monument in the United States. You can ride up inside it and look out over the broad Mississippi River. At the foot of the arch, you can take a ride on an old-fashioned riverboat.

The Gateway Arch

Sea lion at the St. Louis Zoo

★ **St. Louis Zoo:** Highlights of the zoo include a penguin habitat, an **aviary**, and an African Nile exhibit, where you can watch hippos swimming underwater.

★ **Laclede's Landing:** This old riverfront area of St. Louis is filled with cobblestone streets. The old warehouses have been converted into shops and restaurants.

★ **Forest Park:** Created in 1876, this is one of the largest urban parks in the nation. It was the site of the 1904 world's fair.

★ **Cathedral Basilica of St. Louis:** This church contains the world's largest collection of **mosaics**. More than 100 million pieces of glass and stone were used to make the pictures that adorn its walls.

SEE IT HERE!

CITY MUSEUM

City Museum in St. Louis has been called a "sandbox for the inner child." This giant fun house is located in what was once the world's largest shoe factory. The museum's attractions are made entirely out of objects and materials found in St. Louis. The builders used old chimneys, construction cranes, abandoned bridges, and much more to create an out-of-this-world playground where kids can explore crazy caves or climb through a giant Slinky.

★ **Busch Stadium:** St. Louis is crazy for baseball. Check out the madness at Busch Stadium, where the Cardinals play.

★ **American Kennel Club Museum of the Dog:** You'll see a fascinating array of paintings, sculptures, and photographs of dogs at this museum.

WORDS TO KNOW

aviary *a large walk-in enclosure where birds have room to fly*

mosaics *patterns or pictures formed from small pieces of colored tile, glass, or stone*

Missouri Botanical Garden

★ **Missouri Botanical Garden:**
Thousands of plants, including
more than 4,800 trees, grow in this
150-year-old garden.

★ **Laumeier Sculpture Park:** At this
park, you can explore giant outdoor
artwork in a beautiful green setting.

SEE IT HERE!

ST. LOUIS WALK OF FAME

St. Louis has a Walk of Fame that honors famous
residents of the Missouri city. Large brass stars are
embedded in the sidewalks of Delmar Boulevard in the
University City section. Plaques next to each star describe
the life and achievements of each famous resident.
People honored on the St. Louis Walk of Fame range from
baseball player Stan Musial to flight pioneer Charles A.
Lindbergh to movie star Betty Grable.

★ **Washington University in St.
Louis:** In 1904, its buildings were
used as the headquarters of the St.
Louis world's fair.

Bonne Terre

★ **Bonne Terre Mine:** This former
lead mine holds the world's largest
human-made underground lake.
When the mine closed in 1962, the
pumps that had kept it dry for 100
years were turned off. Water began
to fill the mine. Today, deep divers
come to the mine to explore the
watery world.

Imperial

★ **Mastodon State Historic Site:** This
spot just south of St. Louis was once
a swamp. Mastodons, ancient ances-
tors of elephants, sometimes lum-
bered into the swamp and became
trapped. Today, the site preserves a
collection of mastodon bones found
there.

A display at the Mastodon State Historic Site

THE SOUTHEAST

THINGS TO DO: Walk into an old town in Illinois that can be reached only from Missouri, explore Missouri's first permanent European settlement, and learn how Missouri's Native Americans lived.

Ste. Genevieve

★ **Historic buildings:** Walk the streets of Missouri's first permanent European settlement and you'll see the largest collection of French Colonial buildings in North America.

Winter in Ste. Genevieve

New Madrid

★ **New Madrid Historical Museum:** This is the place to learn about the New Madrid earthquakes and Native American mound builders who must have experienced the trembling earth themselves.

★ **Towosahgy State Historic Site:** Here you can see ceremonial mounds built by Mississippian people almost 1,000 years ago. The site's name is an Osage word for "old town."

SEE IT HERE!

KASKASKIA

The French settled the town of Kaskaskia in Illinois in 1703. The town grew and even served as the capital of Illinois Territory from 1809 to 1818. Kaskaskia was located on a small peninsula that jutted out into the Mississippi River. But over time, the river cut a channel through the peninsula. By 1881, the town was stranded on an island. Today, Illinoisans can't get to their former capital without going into Missouri first. The only bridge to Kaskaskia Island is located in St. Mary, Missouri.

CENTRAL MISSOURI

THINGS TO DO: Visit the state capitol, explore the twists and turns of Lake of the Ozarks, or bike along the Missouri River.

Jefferson City

★ **Missouri State Capitol:** On a tour of the capitol, you can watch lawmakers in action. And don't miss Thomas Hart Benton's murals depicting Missouri history.

★ **Jefferson Landing State Historic Site:** This site includes one of the few old hotels located right on a riverboat landing on the Missouri River.

Bagnell

★ **Lake of the Ozarks:** This sprawling lake was created when Bagnell Dam was built. After visiting the dam in the tiny town of Bagnell, explore some of the lake's 1,375 miles (2,213 km) of shoreline.

Lake of the Ozarks

Camdenton

★ **Ha Ha Tonka State Park:** This park's rough terrain is the result of a huge cave system collapsing. You can visit one cavern that features a stalagmite more than 100 feet (30 m) tall.

Columbia

★ **Cosmo Skate Park:** Visit this huge skate park to practice your best moves.

Boonville

★ **Thespian Hall:** Dating to the 1850s, this is the oldest theater in the Mississippi valley. It's still in use today as the Lyric Theater.

★ **Boone's Lick State Historic Site:** Do you like salt on your food? So did early Missourians. You can see how Daniel Boone's sons made salt from mineral springs at this site.

★ **Katy Trail:** Do you have a bike or a great pair of hiking shoes? Then you're ready to take on the Katy Trail. It's a path more than 200 miles (320 km) long across the state along the Missouri River from Machens to Sedalia. The trail is the former path of the Missouri-Kansas-Texas Railroad.

THE OZARKS

THINGS TO DO: Listen to toe-tapping music, see how the Osage people lived, or canoe down a wild river.

Branson

★ **Live music:** Top performers in country and western, Broadway, pop, and more perform in several theaters, as well as on the *Showboat Branson Belle.*

★ **Branson Scenic Railway:** A train takes you through areas of the Ozarks that you can't reach by car.

★ ***Titanic* Museum:** Built to look like the original *Titanic*, this unique museum features some 400 artifacts from the ship and its passengers.

Mansfield

★ **Laura Ingalls Wilder Historic Home and Museum:** Wilder wrote the Little House books here. The museum's exhibits bring pioneer days to life.

Showboat Branson Belle

Diamond

★ **George Washington Carver National Monument:** Visitors can learn about agricultural science and the many uses of peanuts on the farm where George Washington Carver grew up.

MINI-BIO

GEORGE WASHINGTON CARVER: THE PEANUT AND SWEET POTATO MAN

George Washington Carver (1864–1943) was born during the Civil War to an enslaved woman on the Carver farm in Diamond. When he was a baby, Confederate raiders kidnapped him, his mother, and his sister. Only he survived. He was returned to the Carver farm, where his mother's former owners raised him. Carver studied at several colleges in Iowa, where he took up the challenge of helping poor farmers make a living. Years of growing only cotton or only tobacco had worn out the soil. Carver tested alternating cotton with peanuts to make the soil fertile again. This led him to discover more than 300 uses for peanuts. He also discovered more than 100 uses for sweet potatoes.

? **Want to know more?** Visit www.factsfornow .scholastic.com and enter the keyword **Missouri**.

St. Joseph

★ **Pony Express National Museum:**
Here you can visit Pikes Peak
Stables, where the Pony Express
riders left St. Joseph on their race to
California.

Lamar

★ **Harry S Truman Birthplace:**
Missouri's only native-born president was born in this little four-room
house.

★ **Osage Village:** In the 1700s, as
many as 3,000 Osages lived on this
site, which was the center for their
vast fur-trading business. A walking
tour of the area brings Osage history
to life.

Van Buren

★ **Ozark National Scenic Riverways:**
Throughout the year, people enjoy
canoeing down the clear waters of
the Current or Jacks Fork rivers.

Canoeing on the Current River

KANSAS CITY AREA

THINGS TO DO: Learn about
the early days of air travel,
hear great music, or find out
what life was like in the 19th century.

Kansas City

★ **Fort Osage:** Osages and white traders met and traded at this fort until
1819. Today, you can visit the recon-
structed fort to learn about how they
did business.

★ **Nelson-Atkins Museum of Art:**
This museum sits on top of the hill
where newspaper publisher William
Rockhill Nelson built his home.
The museum garden includes the
nation's largest collection of bronze
sculptures by 20th-century British
artist Henry Moore.

★ **Airline History Museum:** This
museum takes you back to the
early days of airlines. You can see
employee uniforms, antique instru-
ments, and old planes.

★ **Crown Center:** This complex
includes shops, hotels, fountains,
live theater, and, in winter, a skat-
ing rink. It was built by Joyce C.
Hall, the founder of Hallmark Cards.
While you're there, take a look at the
Hallmark Visitors Center to learn
how greeting cards are made.

Visitors at the Negro Leagues Baseball Museum

Jackie Robinson was playing with the Kansas City Monarchs, a Negro League team, when he signed with the Brooklyn Dodgers, becoming the first African American in the major leagues.

★ **Negro Leagues Baseball Museum:** Learn about the greatest African American baseball players from the era before major league teams started signing African American players.

★ **American Jazz Museum:** At this museum, you can learn all about jazz and hear great jazz musicians play. Behind the museum is a huge bronze head of jazz giant Charlie Parker, a Kansas City native.

Lexington

★ **Battle of Lexington State Historic Site:** An early battle of the Civil War in Missouri took place here. The damage done by exploding shells is still visible in a mansion on the site.

Lawson

★ **Watkins Woolen Mill State Park:** Costumed guides demonstrate the skills it took to live in 19th-century Missouri. Visitors can try their hand at cutting logs, washing clothes in a tub, or making wooden toys.

Independence

★ **Harry S Truman National Historic Site:** You'll get a glimpse into the private life of the only president born in Missouri when you tour his home in Independence. Much of the house's furnishings remain where the Truman family left them.

★ **Harry S Truman Library & Museum:** You can learn more about Truman's life and times at this museum. The library contains Truman's diaries, letters, and other writings, including important papers explaining his decision to drop the atomic bomb.

SCIENCE, TECHNOLOGY, ENGINEERING, & MATH PROJECTS

Make weather maps, graph population statistics, and research endangered species that live in the state.

120

PRIMARY VS. SECONDARY SOURCES

121

So what are primary and secondary sources? And what's the diff? This section explains all that and where you can find them.

BIOGRAPHICAL DICTIONARY

133

This at-a-glance guide highlights some of the state's most important and influential people. Visit this section and read about their contributions to the state, the country, and the world.

RESOURCES

Books and much more. Take a look at these additional sources for information about the state.

138

WRITING PROJECTS

Write a Memoir, Journal, or Editorial for Your School Newspaper!

Picture Yourself . . .

★ As a Mississippian mound builder. Describe the work that went into building a mound. What motivated the people of your village to build a mound? How would the mound be used?

SEE: Chapter Two, pages 25–26.

★ In Independence preparing to travel the Oregon Trail. What would you do to prepare for such a journey? What does it feel like to be heading into the unknown? Keep a journal describing your experiences.

SEE: Chapter Four, pages 46–48.

Create an Election Brochure or Web Site!

Run for office! In this book, you've read about some of the issues that concern Missouri today. As a candidate for governor of Missouri, create a campaign brochure or Web site.

★ Explain how you meet the qualifications to be governor of Missouri.

★ Talk about the three or four major issues you'll focus on if you're elected.

★ Remember, you'll be responsible for Missouri's budget. How would you spend the taxpayers' money?

SEE: Chapter Seven, pages 91–93.

Create an interview script with a famous person from Missouri!

★ Research various famous Missourians, such as George Washington Carver, Maya Angelou, Sheryl Crow, Harry S Truman, and many others.

★ Based on your research, pick one person you would most like to interview.

★ Write a script of the interview. What questions would you ask? How would this famous person answer? Create a question-and-answer format. You may want to supplement this writing project with a voice-recording dramatization of the interview.

SEE: Chapters Five, Six, and Seven, pages 58–95, and the Biographical Dictionary, pages 133–137.

ART PROJECTS

Create a PowerPoint Presentation or Visitors' Guide

Welcome to Missouri!

Missouri is a great place to visit and to live! From its natural beauty to its bustling cities and historical sites, there's plenty to see and do. In your PowerPoint presentation or brochure, highlight 10 to 15 of Missouri's interesting landmarks. Be sure to include:

★ a map of the state showing where these sites are located

★ photos, illustrations, Web links, natural history facts, geographic stats, climate and weather, plants and wildlife, and recent discoveries

SEE: Chapter Nine, pages 106–115, and Fast Facts, pages 126–127.

Illustrate the Lyrics to the Missouri State Song

("Missouri Waltz")

Use markers, paints, photos, collages, colored pencils, or computer graphics to illustrate the lyrics to "Missouri Waltz." Turn your illustrations into a picture book, or scan them into PowerPoint and add music.

SEE: The lyrics to "Missouri Waltz" on page 128.

Research Missouri's State Quarter

From 1999 to 2008, the U.S. Mint introduced new quarters commemorating each of the 50 states in the order that they were admitted to the Union. Each state's quarter features a unique design on its reverse, or back.

★ Research the significance of the image. Who designed the quarter? Who chose the final design?

★ Design your own Missouri quarter. What images would you choose for the reverse?

★ Make a poster showing the Missouri quarter and label each image.

GO TO: www.factsfornow.scholastic.com. Enter the keyword **Missouri** and look for the link to the Missouri quarter.

SCIENCE, TECHNOLOGY, ENGINEERING, & MATH PROJECTS

Graph Population Statistics!

★ Compare population statistics (such as ethnic background, birth, death, and literacy rates) in Missouri counties or major cities.

★ On your graph or chart, look at population density, and write sentences describing what the population statistics show; graph one set of population statistics, and write a paragraph explaining what the graphs reveal.

SEE: Chapter Six, pages 72–76.

Create a Weather Map of Missouri!

Use your knowledge of Missouri's geography to research and identify conditions that result in specific weather events. What is it about the geography of Missouri that makes it vulnerable to things such as tornadoes? Create a weather map or poster that shows the weather patterns over the state. To accompany your map, explain the technology used to measure weather phenomena and provide data.

SEE: Chapter One, page 18.

Gray wolf

Track Endangered Species

★ Using your knowledge of Missouri's wildlife, research which animals and plants are endangered or threatened. Find out what the state is doing to protect these species.

★ Chart known populations of the animals and plants, and report on changes in certain geographic areas

SEE: Chapter One, pages 18–21.

PRIMARY VS. SECONDARY SOURCES

What's the Diff?

Your teacher may require at least one or two primary sources and one or two secondary sources for your assignment. So, what's the difference between the two?

★ **Primary sources are original.** You are reading the actual words of someone's diary, journal, letter, autobiography, or interview. Primary sources can also be photographs, maps, prints, cartoons, news/film footage, posters, first-person newspaper articles, drawings, musical scores, and recordings. By the way, when you conduct a survey, interview someone, shoot a video, or take photographs to include in a project, you are creating primary sources!

★ **Secondary sources are what you find in encyclopedias, textbooks, articles, biographies, and almanacs.** These are written by a person or group of people who tell about something that happened to someone else. Secondary sources also recount what another person said or did. This book is an example of a secondary source.

Now that you know what primary sources are—where can you find them?

★ **Your school or local library:** Check the library catalog for collections of original writings, government documents, musical scores, and so on. Some of this material may be stored on microfilm.

★ **Historical societies:** These organizations keep historical documents, photographs, and other materials.
Staff members can help you find what you are looking for. History museums are also great places to see primary sources firsthand.

★ **The Internet:** There are lots of sites that have primary sources you can download and use in a project or assignment.

TIMELINE

★ ★ ★

U.S. Events		Missouri Events

1000

c. 1000
Mississippian people begin
building temple mounds.

1400

1492
Christopher Columbus and his crew
sight land in the Caribbean Sea.

1500

1541
Hernando de Soto and his party become
the first Europeans to reach Missouri.

1600

1607
The first permanent English settlement in
North America is established at Jamestown.

1620
Pilgrims found Plymouth Colony, the
second permanent English settlement.

1673
French explorers Jacques Marquette
and Louis Jolliet reach Missouri.

1682
René-Robert Cavelier, Sieur de La Salle,
claims more than 1 million square miles (2.6
million sq km) of territory in the Mississippi
River basin for France, naming it Louisiana.

1700

1715
Slaves are brought into Missouri to mine lead.

1735
Ste. Genevieve becomes the first permanent
European settlement in Missouri.

1764
St. Louis is founded.

1776
Thirteen American colonies declare their
independence from Great Britain.

1787
The U.S. Constitution is written.

St. Louis

U.S. Events `1800` **Missouri Events**

U.S. Events

1803
The Louisiana Purchase almost doubles the size of the United States.

1812–15
The United States and Great Britain fight the War of 1812.

1830
The Indian Removal Act forces eastern Native American groups to relocate west of the Mississippi River.

1846–48
The United States fights a war with Mexico over western territories in the Mexican War.

1861–65
The American Civil War is fought between the Northern Union and the Southern Confederacy; it ends with the surrender of the Confederate army.

1866
The U.S. Congress approves the Fourteenth Amendment to the U.S. Constitution, granting citizenship to African Americans.

Missouri Events

1803
The United States buys Louisiana Territory, which includes Missouri.

1817
The first steamboats arrive in St. Louis.

1820
The Missouri Compromise is reached, allowing Missouri to enter the Union as a Slave State.

1821
Missouri becomes the 24th state; traders open the Santa Fe Trail from Missouri to New Mexico.

1836
Native Americans are forced to leave northwestern Missouri to prepare for the Platte Purchase.

1843
Pioneers begin leaving Missouri along the Oregon Trail.

1857
The Supreme Court rules that enslaved Missourian Dred Scott has no right to sue for his freedom.

Dred Scott

1860
The Pony Express is established to bring mail from Missouri to California.

1865
Missouri becomes the first slaveholding state to end slavery.

U.S. Events   `1900`   Missouri Events

1904
St. Louis hosts a world's fair.

1917–18
The United States engages in World War I.

1920
The Nineteenth Amendment to the U.S. Constitution grants women the right to vote.

1920s
Kansas City becomes a thriving jazz center.

1929
The stock market crashes, plunging the United States more deeply into the Great Depression.

1931
The Lake of the Ozarks is created by Bagnell Dam.

1941–45
The United States engages in World War II.

1945
President Harry Truman orders atomic bombs dropped on two Japanese cities.

1950–53
The United States engages in the Korean War.

1958
Branson begins developing as a tourist center.

1964–73
The United States engages in the Vietnam War.

1968
William Clay is elected Missouri's first African American congressman.

1980
Courts order that Missouri schools desegregate.

1991
The United States and other nations engage in the brief Persian Gulf War against Iraq.

`2000`

2001
Terrorists hijack four U.S. aircraft and crash them into the World Trade Center in New York City, the Pentagon in Arlington, Virginia, and a Pennsylvania field, killing thousands.

2003
The United States and coalition forces invade Iraq.

2011
A tornado strikes Joplin, killing 158 people and injuring about 1,150.

GLOSSARY

abolitionists people who worked to end slavery

archaeologist a person who studies the remains of past human societies

arsenal a place where weapons are made or stored

aviary a large walk-in enclosure where birds have room to fly

ceded gave up or granted

equine related to the horse family

fault a break in the rock deep in the earth along which earthquakes may occur

feminist holding the belief that women are the political, economic, and social equals of men

genes chemicals in plants and animals that determine the traits passed from one generation to the next

glaciers slow-moving masses of ice

guerrilla describing soldiers who don't belong to regular armies; they often use surprise attacks and other uncommon battle tactics

latitude the position of a place, measured in degrees north or south of the equator

levees ridges of land built up along a riverbank to prevent flooding

missionaries people who try to convert others to a religion

mosaics patterns or pictures formed from small pieces of colored tile, glass, or stone

pasteurize to heat a liquid in order to kill germs in it

plateau an elevated part of the earth with steep slopes

repealed withdrawn; canceled

sediment material eroded from rocks and deposited elsewhere by wind, water, or glaciers

sedimentary formed from clay, sand, and gravel that settled at the bottom of a body of water

segregated separated from others, according to race, class, ethnic group, religion, or other factors

temperance moderation, especially in drinking alcoholic beverages

till the gravel and soil left behind after a glacier retreats

transcontinental crossing an entire continent

FAST FACTS

State Symbols

State seal

Statehood date	August 10, 1821, the 24th state
Origin of state name	Mesquakie people called their neighbors *Oumessourit*, meaning "people of the big canoes"
State capital	Jefferson City
State nickname	Show-Me State
State motto	*Salus populi suprema lex esto* (Let the welfare of the people be the supreme law)
State bird	Native bluebird
State flower	White Hawthorn blossom
State rock	Mozarkite
State mineral	Galena (lead ore)
State song	"Missouri Waltz"
State tree	Flowering dogwood
State fair	Sedalia (third week in August)

Geography

Total area; rank	69,702 square miles (180,529 sq km); 21st
Land; rank	68,716 square miles (177,974 sq km); 18th
Water; rank	987 square miles (2,556 sq km); 32nd
Inland water; rank	987 square miles (2,556 sq km); 24th
Geographic center	Miller County, 20 miles (32 km) southwest of Jefferson City
Latitude	36° N to 40°35' N
Longitude	89°6' W to 95°42' W
Highest point	Taum Sauk Mountain, 1,772 feet (540 m), in Iron County
Lowest point	St. Francis River, 230 feet (70 m), in Dunklin County
Largest city	Kansas City
Number of counties	114, plus independent city of St. Louis
Longest river	Missouri River, 175 miles (282 km) in Missouri

Population

Population; rank (2010 census)	5,988,927; 18th
Density (2010 census)	87 persons per square mile (34 per sq km)
Population distribution (2010 census)	70% urban, 30% rural
Ethnic distribution (2010 census)	White persons: 81.0%
	Black persons: 11.5%
	Persons of Hispanic or Latino origin: 3.5%
	Persons reporting two or more races: 1.8%
	Asian persons: 1.6%
	American Indian and Alaska Native persons: 0.4%
	Native Hawaiian and other Pacific Islanders: 0.1%
	Persons of some other race: 0.1%

Weather

Record high temperature	118°F (48°C) at Union and Warsaw on July 14, 1954
Record low temperature	−40°F (−40°C) at Warsaw on February 13, 1905
Average July temperature, St. Louis	80°F (27°C)
Average January temperature, St. Louis	32°F (0°C)
Average yearly precipitation, St. Louis	41 inches (104 cm)

State flag

STATE SONG

★ ★ ★

"Missouri Waltz"

"Missouri Waltz" became the state song on June 30, 1949. The origin of the song is unclear, although historians generally agree Frederick Knight Logan first printed it around 1912 after obtaining the melody from orchestra leader John Valentine Eppel. In 1914, the Forster Publishing Company bought the rights to the melody. Jim Shannon added lyrics. The song became popular when Harry Truman was president. He often played the tune on the White House piano.

Hush-a-bye, ma baby, slumbertime is comin' soon;
Rest yo' head upon my breast while Mommy hums a tune;
The sandman is callin' where shadows are fallin',
While the soft breezes sigh as in days long gone by.

Way down in Missouri where I heard this melody,
When I was a little child upon my Mommy's knee;
The old folks were hummin'; their banjoes were strummin';
So sweet and low.

Strum, strum, strum, strum, strum,
Seems I hear those banjoes playin' once again,
Hum, hum, hum, hum, hum,
That same old plaintive strain.

Hear that mournful melody,
It just haunts you the whole day long,
And you wander in dreams back to Dixie, it seems,
When you hear that old time song.

Hush-a-bye, ma baby, go to sleep on Mommy's knee,
Journey back to Dixieland in dreams again with me;
It seems like your Mommy is there once again,
And the old folks were strummin' that same old refrain.

Way down in Missouri where I learned this lullaby,
When the stars were blinkin' and the moon was climbin' high,
Seems I hear voices low, as in days long ago,
Singin' hush-a-bye.

NATURAL AREAS AND HISTORIC SITES

★ ★ ★

National Monument

Missouri is home to one national monument, the *George Washington Carver National Monument*, which features the hills, woodlands, and prairies surrounding the boyhood home of Carver, an African American botanist.

National Scenic Riverways

The *Ozark National Scenic Riverways* is the state's only national scenic riverway system. Visitors can canoe, swim, and fish in the clear waters of the Current and Jacks Fork rivers. They can also explore caves and bluffs and enjoy diverse plant and animal life.

National Expansion Memorial

The *Jefferson National Expansion Memorial* features the Gateway Arch, the Museum of Westward Expansion, and St. Louis's Old Courthouse, all in celebration of the spirit of the western pioneers.

National Battlefield

Wilson's Creek National Battlefield commemorates the first major battle of the Civil War fought west of the Mississippi River.

National Historic Sites

The *Harry S Truman National Historic Site* includes the home where the 33rd president lived from 1919 until his death and the family farm he worked on as a young man.

The *Ulysses S. Grant National Historic Site* features the house, barn, icehouse, and other buildings on the farm where Grant lived for part of his adult life. The site commemorates the 18th president's life, military career, and presidency.

National Historic Trails

Six national historic trails cross Missouri. They are the *California National Historic Trail;* the *Lewis & Clark National Historic Trail;* the *Oregon National Historic Trail;* the *Pony Express National Historic Trail;* the *Santa Fe National Historic Trail;* and the *Trail of Tears National Historic Trail.*

State Parks and Forests

Missouri's state park system features more than 50 state parks, including *Big Lake State Park, Elephant Rocks State Park, Onondaga Cave State Park,* and *Route 66 State Park.*

SPORTS TEAMS

★ ★ ★

NCAA Teams (Division I)

Missouri State University *Bears*
Southeast Missouri State University *Redhawks*
St. Louis University *Billikens*
University of Missouri–Columbia *Tigers*
University of Missouri–Kansas City *Kangaroos*

PROFESSIONAL SPORTS TEAMS

★ ★ ★

Major League Baseball

Kansas City *Royals*
St. Louis *Cardinals*

National Hockey League

St. Louis *Blues*

National Football League

Kansas City *Chiefs*
St. Louis *Rams*

Major League Soccer

Kansas City *Wizards*

CULTURAL INSTITUTIONS

Libraries

The *Harry S. Truman Library & Museum* in Independence is part of the Harry S Truman National Historic Site. It contains more than 3 million documents from Truman's presidency.

The *Missouri State Library*, built in 1946 in Jefferson City, holds the state archives.

The *Pius XII Memorial Library* at St. Louis University has a collection of microfilmed documents from the Vatican Library, the library of the Roman Catholic Church.

Museums

The *Magic House–St. Louis Children's Museum* (St. Louis) is dedicated to providing hands-on learning experiences for children.

The *Missouri History Museum* (St. Louis) features exhibits on the history of Missouri.

The *Museum of Westward Expansion* (St. Louis) explores the history of Native Americans and the pioneers who crossed North America.

The *Nelson-Atkins Museum of Art* (Kansas City) is one of the 10 largest art museums in the United States. It has a notable collection of East Asian art.

The *St. Louis Art Museum* is home to 30,000 works of art, including a 3,000-year-old Egyptian mummy.

The *St. Louis Science Center* encourages an understanding of the environment, humanity, technology, and space sciences.

The *Toy and Miniature Museum of Kansas City* has 38 rooms filled with antique dolls, dollhouses, toys, and trains.

Performing Arts

The *Kansas City Symphony* was formed in 1982. The symphony employs 80 full-time musicians and stages performances 42 weeks each year.

Opera Theatre of Saint Louis is an opera festival that presents four operas each summer. The performances are accompanied by the Saint Louis Symphony Orchestra.

Universities and Colleges

In 2011, Missouri had 14 public and 77 private institutions of higher learning.

ANNUAL EVENTS

January–March

Taste of Soulard in St. Louis (February)

True/False Film Fest in Columbia (February–March)

St. Patrick's Day Parade in Kansas City (March)

Wurstfest in Hermann (March)

April–June

Big Muddy Folk Festival in Boonville (April)

Dogwood Festival in Camdenton (April)

Maifest in Hermann (May)

St. Louis Storytelling Festival in St. Louis (May)

Valley of Flowers Festival in Florissant (May)

Scott Joplin Ragtime Festival in Sedalia (June)

July–September

National Tom Sawyer Days in Hannibal (July)

Fair St. Louis (July)

Jour de Fete (Festival Day) in Ste. Genevieve (August)

Missouri State Fair in Sedalia (August)

Ozark Empire Fair in Springfield (August)

Cotton Carnival in Sikeston (September)

Country Club Plaza Art Fair in Kansas City (September)

Great Forest Park Balloon Race in St. Louis (September)

October–December

Fête d'Automne in Old Mines (October)

Oktoberfest in Hermann (October)

Pony Express PumpkinFest in St. Joseph (October)

Ozark Mountain Christmas in Branson (November–December)

BIOGRAPHICAL DICTIONARY

Zoë Akins (1886–1958) was a poet and playwright born in Humansville. She won the 1935 Pulitzer Prize for her play *The Old Maid*.

Robert Altman (1925–2006) was a film director who made movies such as *McCabe & Mrs. Miller*, *M*A*S*H**, and *Nashville*. He was born in Kansas City.

Maya Angelou See page 85.

Henry Armstrong (1912–1988) was a world boxing champion raised in St. Louis. He was the only boxer to hold three world championships at the same time.

Josephine Baker See page 82.

Count Basie (1904–1984) was a pianist, bandleader, and composer who helped make Kansas City a jazz center.

Tom Bass (1859–1934), who was born into slavery near Columbia, was one of the world's greatest horse trainers.

Maya Angelou

Thomas Hart Benton (1889–1975) was an artist who often painted idealized images of rural America. Born in Neosho, he was the son of a Missouri congressman and great-nephew of Missouri's first senator.

Yogi Berra (1925–) was a longtime catcher for the New York Yankees. He later became a manager, leading both the New York Mets and the Yankees to World Series championships. He was born in St. Louis.

Chuck Berry (1926–) is a pioneer of rock and roll who wrote and performed songs such as "Johnny B. Goode" and "Roll Over Beethoven." He was born in Overland.

Susan Blow See page 77.

Lucile Bluford See page 68.

Daniel Boone See page 36.

Chuck Berry

Omar N. Bradley (1893–1981) was a U.S. Army general who led troops in North Africa and Europe during World War II. He later became the chairman of the Joint Chiefs of Staff, the principal military adviser to the president.

Joe Buck (1969–), born in Florida and raised in St. Louis, is one of America's most famous sports announcers. He is the son of the legendary sportscaster Jack Buck, who announced St. Louis Cardinals baseball games on radio and television for 47 years.

Martha Jane Cannary (Calamity Jane) See page 56.

Kit Carson (1809–1868) was a legendary guide in the American West. He also led military actions against the Navajo people, forcing them on a march across New Mexico. He was born in Franklin.

George Washington Carver See page 113.

Kate Chopin (1850–1904) wrote the early feminist novel *The Awakening*. She was born in St. Louis.

Walter Cronkite

William Clark (1770–1838), along with Meriwether Lewis, led the expedition to explore the Louisiana Purchase. He later served as governor of the Missouri Territory.

Walter Cronkite (1916–2009) was the anchorman of the *CBS Evening News* for 19 years. He was often called "the most trusted man in America" because of his vast journalistic experience and his serious yet kindly manner. He was born in St. Joseph.

Sheryl Crow (1962–) is a Grammy Award–winning rock singer, songwriter, and guitarist. She is a native of Kennett.

Walt Disney See page 80.

Thomas Stearns (T. S.) Eliot (1888–1965) was a pioneer of modern poetry whose works include *The Waste Land* and *"The Love Song of J. Alfred Prufrock."* Born in St. Louis, he was awarded the Nobel Prize in Literature.

John Goodman (1952–) is an actor known for his role as Dan Conner on the TV series *Roseanne* and his performances in such movies as *Inside Llewyn Davis*, *The Flintstones*, and *The Big Lebowski*. He was born in St. Louis.

John Goodman

Betty Grable (1916–1973) was a top movie star of the 1940s who appeared in films such as *Moon over Miami* and *Tin Pan Alley*. She was born in St. Louis.

Joyce C. Hall See page 102.

William Least Heat-Moon (1940–) is a travel writer who writes about small-town and rural America. His works include *Blue Highways* and *PrairyErth*. Part Osage, Irish, and English, he was born in Kansas City.

Robert Heinlein (1907–1988), who was born in Butler, has been called the "dean of science fiction writers." His novels include *Stranger in a Strange Land*, *Starship Troopers*, and *I Will Fear No Evil*. Many of his novels and short stories deal with social issues such as religion, politics, race, and freedom.

Edwin P. Hubble (1889–1953) was an astronomer who discovered that the universe is expanding. His ideas were used in developing the Big Bang theory of the origins of the universe. He was born in Marshfield.

William Least Heat-Moon

Langston Hughes

Langston Hughes (1902–1967) was a poet, playwright, novelist, and newspaper columnist whose work explored African American life. He was born in Joplin.

John Huston (1906–1987) was a film director and screenwriter. His classic films include *The Maltese Falcon*, *Key Largo*, *The Asphalt Jungle*, and *The Treasure of the Sierra Madre*, for which he won two Oscar Awards. He was born in Nevada, Missouri.

Scott Joplin See page 81.

William Lear (1902–1978) was an inventor and businessman. He founded the Lear Jet Corporation, a manufacturer of jets used to transport small groups of people. He was born in Hannibal.

Jim Lee (1964–) is a comic book writer and artist who has worked on superhero characters such as the X-Men, WildC.A.T.s, and Batman. Born in Seoul, South Korea, he grew up in St. Louis.

Meriwether Lewis (1774–1809), with William Clark, led the expedition to explore the Louisiana Purchase. He later served as governor of the Louisiana Territory and lived in St. Louis.

Stan Musial

Elijah P. Lovejoy (1802–1837) was the editor of a newspaper published in St. Louis. He was murdered for his abolitionist views.

Alexander McNair See page 45.

Marianne Moore (1887–1972) was a leading poet of the 20th century. Her *Collected Poems* of 1951 won the Pulitzer Prize and the National Book Award.

Stan Musial (1920–2013) played for the St. Louis Cardinals for 22 years. He led the National League in batting average seven times in his career and was inducted into the Baseball Hall of Fame in 1969.

Carry Nation See page 62.

Nelly (Cornell Haynes Jr.) (1974–), who grew up in St. Louis, is one of the best-selling rap singers of all time. His hits include "Hot in Here" and "Dilemma."

Rose O'Neill (1874–1944), a longtime resident of Missouri, was an artist and illustrator. She is best known for creating the Kewpie characters, which gained fame in cartoons and as porcelain toys known as Kewpie dolls.

Charlie Parker (1920–1955) was one of the most influential jazz saxophonists and composers of all time. He was instrumental in developing the bebop style of jazz, which features fast tempos, complex harmonies, and frequent improvisations. He grew up in Kansas City.

Thomas Pendergast See page 63.

Marlin Perkins (1905–1986) was a zoologist, the head of the St. Louis Zoo, and the host of the TV program *Wild Kingdom* from 1963 to 1984. He was born in Carthage.

John Pershing See page 61.

Brad Pitt (1963–) is one of the most popular actors in Hollywood. He has appeared in films such as *A River Runs Through It*, *Legends of the Fall*, and *Ocean's Eleven*. He grew up in Springfield.

Vincent Price (1911–1993) was an actor who appeared in many horror films, including *The Fly*, *House of Usher*, and *The Raven*. He was born in St. Louis.

Joseph Pulitzer (1847–1911) was the publisher of the *St. Louis Post-Dispatch*; he established the Pulitzer Prizes.

Spotswood Rice See page 54.

Brad Pitt

Mona Van Duyn

Nellie Tayloe Ross (1876–1977), a native of St. Joseph, was the first female governor in the nation's history. She became governor of Wyoming in 1925.

Charles M. Russell (1864–1926) was a painter and sculptor best known for his scenes of the American West. He was born in St. Louis.

Phyllis Schlafly (1924–) is an author and activist known for her conservative political views. Born in St. Louis, she has written more than 20 books on topics such as child care and women's issues.

Charles "Casey" Stengel See page 87.

Sara Teasdale (1884–1933), born in St. Louis, was a Pulitzer Prize–winning poet whose short, personal lyrics are noted for their simplicity and romantic subject matter.

Harry S Truman See page 93.

Mark Twain See page 83.

Mona Van Duyn (1921–2004) was a poet who taught at Washington University in St. Louis for many years. She was the nation's first female poet laureate.

Mort Walker (1923–) is a cartoonist who created the comic strips *Beetle Bailey* and *Hi and Lois*. He was raised in Kansas City.

Sam Walton (1918–1992) was born in Oklahoma and grew up in Shelbina and Columbia, Missouri, where he attended the University of Missouri as a military cadet. He founded the Walmart and Sam's Club stores.

Tom Watson (1949–) was one of the world's leading golfers in the 1970s and 1980s. Watson won eight major championships, including five Open Championships, two Masters Tournaments, and one U.S. Open. He was born in Kansas City.

Laura Ingalls Wilder (1867–1957) moved with her pioneer family from Wisconsin to Minnesota, Iowa, and the Dakotas. As an adult, she settled in Mansfield, Missouri, where she worked as a newspaper columnist and wrote books about her childhood. These books, such as *Little House on the Prairie* and *On the Banks of Plum Creek*, have become classics of children's literature.

Tennessee Williams (1911–1983) was a playwright who wrote the classic dramas *A Streetcar Named Desire*, *The Glass Menagerie*, and *Cat on a Hot Tin Roof*. He spent much of his childhood in St. Louis.

Laura Ingalls Wilder

RESOURCES

BOOKS

Nonfiction

Abrams, Dennis. *George Washington Carver: Scientist and Educator*. New York: Chelsea House, 2008.

Benoit, Peter. *The Trail of Tears*. New York: Children's Press, 2012.

Friedman, Mel. *The Oregon Trail*. New York: Children's Press, 2013.

Jeffrey, Gary. *The Pony Express*. New York: Gareth Stevens Publishing, 2012.

McNeese, Tim. *Dred Scott v. Sandford: The Pursuit of Freedom*. New York: Chelsea House, 2007.

Miller, Brandon Marie. *Women of the Frontier: 16 Tails of Trailblazing Homesteaders, Entrepreneurs, and Rabble-Rousers*. Chicago: Chicago Review Press, 2012.

Santella, Andrew. *The French and Indian War*. New York: Children's Press, 2012.

Woog, Adam. *Calamity Jane*. New York: Chelsea House, 2010.

Young, Jeff C. *Hernando de Soto: Spanish Conquistador in the Americas*. Berkeley Heights, N.J.: Enslow Publishers, 2009.

Fiction

Ambrose, Stephen. *This Vast Land: A Young Man's Journal of the Lewis and Clark Expedition*. New York: Simon & Schuster, 2003.

Jackson, Louise A. *Exiled: From Tragedy to Triumph on the Missouri Frontier*. Austin, Tex.: Eakin Press, 2007.

Twain, Mark. *The Adventures of Tom Sawyer*. New York: Penguin, 2006. First published 1876.

FACTS FOR NOW

Visit this Scholastic Web site for more information on Missouri:
www.factsfornow.scholastic.com
Enter the keyword **Missouri**

INDEX

★ ★ ★

AUTHOR'S TIPS AND SOURCE NOTES

★　★　★

I used the resources at the Wisconsin State Historical Society while research-ing this book. It has one of the best book collections about North America available anywhere. Among the books I counted on was *Missouri: A Guide to the "Show Me" State*. This book was written during the Great Depression, when the federal government hired writers to produce a book about each state. Filled with historical and travel details, these books continue to be a valuable resource for writers today. *Missouri Then and Now*, by Perry McCandless and William E. Foley, was equally useful.

Of course, I used the Internet, too. Particularly helpful was the Missouri state archives site, where you can read about everything from the history of dueling in Missouri to the effects of the Dred Scott decision.